**A DUCKS UNLIMITED
GUIDE TO**

HUNTING DIVING DUCKS
& SEA DUCKS

by Gary Kramer

DUCKS
UNLIMITED
Memphis, Tennessee

Ducks Unlimited, Inc., and colophon are registered trademarks of Ducks Unlimited, Inc.

Edited by Doug Truax
Art direction by Michael Todd
Book design by Lisa Malone

Published by Ducks Unlimited, Inc.
John A. Tomke, President
D. A. (Don) Young, Executive Vice President

ISBN: 1-932052-10-0
Published September 2003

Ducks Unlimited, Inc.
Ducks Unlimited conserves, restores, and manages wetlands and associated habitats for North America's waterfowl. These habitats also benefit other wildlife and people.

Since its founding in 1937, DU has raised more than $1.6 billion, which has contributed to the conservation of more than 10 million acres of prime wildlife habitat in all 50 states, each of the Canadian provinces, and in key areas of Mexico. In the U.S. alone, DU has helped to conserve over 2 million acres of waterfowl habitat. Some 900 species of wildlife live and flourish on DU projects, including many threatened and endangered species.

Call to Action
The success of Ducks Unlimited hinges upon each member's personal involvement in the conservation of North America's wetlands and waterfowl. You can help Ducks Unlimited meet its conservation goals by volunteering your time, energy, and resources; by participating in our conservation programs; and by encouraging others to do the same. To learn more about how you can make a difference for the ducks, call 1-800-45-DUCKS.

Distributed by The Globe Pequot Press, P.O. Box 480, Guilford, CT 06437-0480.

> *To Eileen, Elaine, and Kelly*

ACKNOWLEDGMENTS

Writing a book is a monumental task that takes perseverance and research. However, when the subject matter is something you enjoy, it becomes easier. It's also an easier task when biologists, guides, and fellow hunters cheerfully agree to provide information. Without their help, this book would not have been possible.

First, I would like to thank the many guides I hunted with and interviewed. They did their best to deliver quality hunts and were honest in their desire to provide useful information. I would particularly like to thank Capt. Jeff Coats for his assistance. Greg Mensik, a fellow biologist and hunter, took the time to review the manuscript, while Dave Paullin, a friend and avid hunter, reviewed the Scouting and the Shotguns and Loads chapters.

I also would like to thank Ducks Unlimited and Chuck Petrie for asking me to write this book in the first place and Art DeLauier Jr. for his encouragement along the way. Additionally, my office assistant, Judy Taylor, has played a key role in managing my office, allowing me to take on long-term projects. I would also like to thank Vince Bruccolieri, Larry Rauen, Ken Mayer, Alan Sands, and Bill Gundy— the guys I started hunting with and still hunt with today—not only for sharing blinds and boats with me, but for being tolerant of my stopping to take photos when we should have been hunting.

Finally, I would like to thank my wife, Eileen, for her understanding of my frequent absences, not only during the course of writing this book but also during our thirty-year marriage. Lastly, my daughters, Elaine and Kelly, have been supportive and accepting of my chosen careers.

CONTENTS

PREFACE vi

INTRODUCTION...ix

1. DIVING & SEA DUCKS: AN OVERVIEW

Natural History 1

History of Diver and Sea Duck Hunting 15

Diver and Sea Duck Hunting Today 22

2. TOP TEN DIVER & SEA DUCK HUNTING DESTINATIONS..29

Lake of the Woods, Minnesota and Ontario 30

Long Point, Ontario 33

Upper Mississippi River, Wisconsin and Iowa 36

Kodiak Island, Alaska 39

The Down East Coast of Maine...............................43

Puget Sound, Washington 46

Chesapeake Bay, Maryland 48

Pamlico Sound, North Carolina..............................52

Catahoula Lake, Louisiana..................................55

Laguna Madre, Texas and Mexico 57

Other Destinations 61

3. HUNTING TACTICS 65
Hunting Marshes and Swamps.............67
Hunting Lakes and Reservoirs 72
Hunting Rivers 81
Hunting Coastal Estuaries and Bays.............86
Layout Boat and Sink Box Hunting.............95
Scull Boat and Sneak Boat Hunting.............100
Pass-Shooting and Jump-Shooting.............104

4. DECOYS, RIGGING, AND CALLING 107
Decoys: Types, Sizes, and Species 109
Decoy Rigging 119
Decoy Spreads 127
Calling Diving and Sea Ducks 142

5. DUCK BLINDS.............149
Permanent Blinds.............153
Portable Blinds.............160
Boat Blinds 163

6. SCOUTING 169

7. SHOTGUNS AND LOADS 179
Shotgun Actions 180
Gauges, Loads, and Chokes 182
Other Shotgun Features.............188
Improving Your Shooting Skill.............192

8. PLANNING A DUCK HUNTING TRIP.............197

PREFACE

I have been interested in the outdoors and wildlife as long as I can remember. Even though there were not many wild places near Los Angeles in the 1960s, I still managed to find a few sparrows and rabbits in vacant lots to shoot with my pellet gun and caught gopher snakes and frogs to bring home. I developed a more refined interest in hunting when I got my driver's license. About that time, my buddies and I graduated from pellet guns and vacant lots to 20-gauges and doves in the southern California deserts.

My interest in duck hunting took a quantum leap in high school, and by the time I was in my early twenties, I had started hunting diving ducks. A stint in the U.S. Navy during the Vietnam War slowed my hunting activity, but when I got out and enrolled in college, I resumed my pursuit of what had become a passion. While in the navy I discovered colleges offered a degree specializing in wildlife management. Humboldt State University had a good program and I applied while still in the service. In 1970, I enrolled in college and in 1974 graduated from Humboldt State University with a B.S. degree in wildlife management. In 1976 I received a master's degree from Humboldt. Upon graduation, I was lucky enough to land a job with the Bureau of Land Management in Ely, Nevada. After eighteen months, I transferred to the U.S. Fish and Wildlife Service as a wildlife biologist at the Kern National Wildlife Refuge northwest of Bakersfield, California.

I wrote my first outdoor story in the late 1970s. It was on brant hunting at San Quintin Bay in Baja California where I had done my master's degree on the same subject a few years earlier. It wasn't long until I had published a second and a third article, and I was on my way to a second career in outdoor writing. In the meantime, I moved from Kern to San Luis National Wildlife Refuge in Los Banos. In 1984, I was selected for my first refuge manager position at Salton Sea National Wildlife Refuge. Along the way I continued to hunt diving ducks whenever I could, all the time refining my equipment, knowledge, and techniques.

My writing expanded to include hunting trips to Argentina and Canada and fishing trips to Mexico and Alaska. I had the best of both worlds—I was involved in wildlife conservation on a daily basis and had a second job as an outdoor writer and photographer. In 1989, I became the refuge manager at Sacramento National Wildlife Refuge near Willows, California. By then I was writing and photographing regularly for *Ducks Unlimited* magazine, *The Bird Hunting Report, Shooting Sportsman, Outdoor Life, American Hunter,* and other national publications. I had the best of both worlds but it was a busy one.

In 1999, the opportunity for an early retirement from the U.S. Fish and Wildlife Service became available, and after plenty of thought I gave up a twenty-six-year government career. One of the first things that came up was an offer from Chuck Petrie at Ducks Unlimited to write a book on diver and sea duck hunting. I jumped at the chance and have spent the past two years gathering information and taking a firsthand look at diver and sea duck hunting across North America.

I have been a student of waterfowl biology and waterfowl hunting for more than thirty years. I have enjoyed my time as a wildlife biologist and refuge manager, as well as my time with a shotgun and camera as an outdoor writer and photographer. Along the way, I have hunted divers and sea ducks from coast to coast and tundra to tropics, yet I do not classify myself as an expert on the subject. After doing the research, making the trips, and writing this book, I am more knowledgeable about diver and sea duck hunting than I was before and, I hope, a better hunter for it. It has brought me even closer to the allure of diver and sea duck hunting, and now I know more than ever why this particular brand of duck hunting is so appealing, especially to hunters who like classic waterfowling and appreciate the importance of the correct equipment and gear.

I hope that by sharing more than thirty years of hunting experience and insight, this book will help you become a better and more efficient diver and sea duck hunter. But equally as important, I hope you better understand the special place diver and sea duck hunting has in our waterfowl heritage and waterfowling today.

Gary Kramer
Willows, California

INTRODUCTION

As a native Californian growing up near Los Angeles, duck hunting might have been the furthest thing from my teenage mind. There's no doubt that by the time I was sixteen and able to drive, girls and cars were on the top of my list, but hunting doves and jackrabbits in the desert occupied several weekends each year. It wasn't until I was eighteen and started hunting ducks that I became a hunting fanatic.

The Mendota Wildlife Area is a five-hour drive north of Los Angeles. One weekend in the mid 1960s, two buddies and I decided to make the trek north to try duck hunting. We knew very little about the mechanics of the sport, but from reading *Sports Afield* and *Outdoor Life,* we did figure out that it would probably help to bring a few decoys and to leave our bright-colored clothes at home. We borrowed a dozen decoys, scrounged up some knee boots, jumped in my 1955 Ford, and headed north toward Fresno. We arrived late at night and crashed in the car until they started checking people into the wildlife area at 4:00 A.M. We didn't have a clue as to where to go or what to do but managed to pester one of the employees to the point he felt sorry for the trio of city kids from L.A. He pointed us in the direction of a wetland on the far side of the area. We followed his instructions, walked out into the marsh, set up the decoys, then tried our best to hide in the cattails. By the time the sun peaked over the horizon, we had gone over the tops of our knee boots, leaving us chilled to the bone, and we managed to miss the only pair of the ducks that were foolish enough to fly by. But we toughed it out for two more hours, and by the time cold and hunger forced us back to the vehicle, we had five ducks between us—one mallard, one pintail, and three green-winged teal. Perhaps not a monumental accomplishment, but to us it was huge and we were proud to join the ranks of that group of hunters known as waterfowlers.

From that day on, I was hooked on waterfowl hunting. It wasn't until several years later, however, that I was introduced to diving ducks. In 1968, I joined the navy and for a short time was stationed at Treasure Island in San Francisco Bay. One day while standing watch early in the morning, I noticed long strings of ducks winging their way across the bay, headed for some distant location. When I mentioned my sighting to one of the sailors in my barracks, he told me he had a cousin who hunted ducks on the bay all the time. I asked if there was any chance of setting up a hunting trip. Several weeks later we left the base in the dark, weaving our way through the city and over the Golden Gate Bridge. Eventually we arrived at a launch ramp near San Rafael where we met Bob's cousin Bill. After introductions, we loaded our gear in the 16-foot aluminum boat and were off.

The damp, salt-laden air hit me square in the face as Bill gunned the outboard and headed across the flooded tide flats. Only the shadowy form of my hunting partner and Bill's Labrador retriever were visible sitting amidships in the predawn darkness. The monotonous drone of the outboard obscured all other sounds as the boat skimmed over a light chop. As I contemplated what this day would bring, I pulled on my gloves and tightened the drawstring on my hood to ward off the cold spray. The dog sat immobile but tense, instinct signaling the beginning of another waterfowling adventure.

Twenty minutes later, a dark form loomed ahead and Bill backed off the throttle, coasting to a stop at the bottom of the huge structure, which turned out to be a stilt blind in the middle of San Pablo Bay.

The blind was a grand affair with space for up to four hunters, a dog, and a place to hide the boat. His grandfather built the blind in the 1940s and his family had maintained it ever since. Bill explained the blind was in an area frequented by canvasbacks and bluebills (scaup). The blind was placed to intercept the birds as they moved on the falling tide from open-water rafting areas to feeding areas.

We put guns, shells, lunches, and the dog in the blind, then went about the task of setting out 100 canvasback and bluebill decoys. They were set in lines of 10 decoys per string, with large weights at both ends to hold them in place against the current. With the decoys in place, we returned to the blind just as the sun peaked over the horizon. All of a sudden Bill pointed to the east as out of the sun came a tight knot of 2 dozen ducks flying at a speed that brought them to the decoys quicker than I had anticipated. "Now," Bill called out and all three of us instinctively stood up and fired. I emptied my Remington 870 pump, dropping one of the four scaup (bluebills) that ended up lying in the decoys. Bob fired one more shot to dispatch a drake that was diving in an attempt to escape. The dog was sent and soon I was admiring a drake scaup—the first diving duck I had ever bagged.

The rest of the morning was picture perfect for divers—a stiff breeze out of the north rippled the surface of the bay just enough to keep the birds flying, and the birds decoyed like nothing I had ever seen before. I had already learned to appreciate mallards dropping "cupped and webbed" into the decoys, and pintails circling in wide passes before deciding it was safe to join the imposters below. But I had never witnessed the spectacle of 3 dozen feathered bombshells approaching low over the water at top speed, and then putting on the brakes to land on the first pass. The experience of setting out masses of decoys, the speed of the birds, how they came to the blocks in large flocks, and the preparation and effort required to successfully hunt them piqued my interest in hunting diving ducks. While I enjoy hunting puddle ducks, I can't help but appreciate and gravitate toward divers and sea ducks for the unique brand of shooting they provide.

Over the past thirty years, I've had the good fortune to hunt diving and sea ducks throughout the United States, Canada, Mexico, and several foreign countries. Yet each morning that I get up at the crack of dawn for a diver or sea duck hunt, some of the excitement I felt that very first day on San Pablo Bay comes alive. I believe a flock of redheads or canvasbacks, boosted by a fifteen-mile-per-hour tailwind and coming full tilt toward the decoys, is among the most spectacular sights waterfowling can deliver.

This book is intended to provide both the casual and serious waterfowler with some insight into diving and sea duck hunting and to celebrate the effort, dedication, and camaraderie that go into a duck hunt. I hope this book will help you to be a more successful diver and sea duck hunter by providing information on the history of the sport, hunting tactics, calling, decoys, blinds, shotguns, and some of the top diver and sea duck hunting destinations in North America. If you are not already hooked on this style of hunting, I hope you will be by the time you finished reading these pages.

Chapter One

DIVING & SEA DUCKS

An Overview

Natural History

Under the scientific classification scheme, all waterfowl (ducks, geese, and swans) belong to the family Anatidae. Puddle ducks, also called dabbling ducks, belong to the tribe Anatini, and they are by far the most familiar group to hunters and the casual observers who throw breadcrumbs to ducks in city parks. The ten species of dabbling ducks include the ubiquitous mallard, the elegant pintail, various species of teal, and others that are all closely related. While their ecological requirements are different, their lifestyles are remarkably similar. The strikingly beautiful wood duck is a member of a group known as perching ducks. They, too, are considered puddle ducks, sharing many characteristics found in the other dabblers.

In contrast, the diving ducks are a strange lot. With three major branches on their family tree, each tribe differs significantly in anatomy, behavior, and habitat requirements. The tribe Aythyini includes the freshwater diving ducks and pochards and has fifteen species worldwide. This group is represented in North America by canvasbacks, redheads, ring-necked ducks, greater scaup, and lesser scaup. The tribe Mergini includes the sea ducks and mergansers, with twenty species worldwide. This large and diverse group includes common eiders, king eiders, spectacled eiders, Steller's eiders, harlequin ducks, oldsquaw (now called long-tailed ducks), black scoters, surf scoters, white-winged scoters, bufflehead, Barrow's goldeneyes, common goldeneyes, hooded mergansers, red-breasted mergansers, and common mergansers. Finally, the tribe Oxyurini, or stiff-tailed ducks, has eight species worldwide, but there are only two in North America—the ruddy duck and masked duck.

For detailed reviews of these species refer to *Duck Country,* written by Michael Furtman and published by Ducks Unlimited. This book provides in-depth information about North American ducks and their natural history.

Both spectacled and Steller's eiders are currently on the federal endangered species list and cannot be killed under any circumstances. Masked ducks are found only in south Texas in limited numbers and, therefore, are not considered a game species. Several other species of diving ducks, most notably canvasbacks, go through population fluctuations that sometimes result in a closed hunting season. Once the population bounces back the season is reopened.

The highly prized canvasback (foreground) is North America's least numerous, most protected diving duck.

"Divers" derive their name from their primary method of feeding, which is diving below the surface of the water. That's not to imply that divers cannot or do not feed on the surface; it means simply that the majority of their food resources are reached by diving. They have a compact and streamlined body. The feet of divers and sea ducks are large, spread wide apart, and placed farther back on the body than on puddle ducks, rendering them less adept at walking on land. Their musculature is different, as well; it is designed for diving rather than rapid takeoffs.

Redheads and other diving ducks sit lower in the water than do their dabbling cousins, compressing their body feathers to expel trapped air prior to diving.

Puddle ducks are able to spring from the water when flushed, while diving and sea ducks require some distance to take off, running along the surface to become airborne. Additionally, the wings of diving and sea ducks are smaller than you will find in an equivalent-sized puddle duck. Once in flight, the running start and shorter wings are not a hindrance. The truth is, most divers and sea ducks fly at about the same speed as puddle ducks, but because their wings are smaller, they must beat them faster to stay airborne, making them appear to be moving faster than they are. Also, divers often approach the decoys at a low angle over the water or drop from towering heights in a single pass, giving the appearance that they are moving at afterburner speed. I still think a flock of canvasbacks dropping out of the sky and over the decoys almost before you can click off the safety is a sight that can't help but take your breath away. Among both dabblers and divers, the canvasback is considered the fastest flyer, reaching speeds of up to 70 miles per hour.

Most divers and sea ducks follow a pattern that includes feeding periods in the morning and in the afternoon. The midday period is spent loafing, often in flocks on large bodies of water. These rafting flocks can be large, numbering from several hundred to several thousand. Researchers on the Upper Mississippi River have observed rafting flocks that exceeded 200,000 birds, mostly canvasbacks. However, most local flights are in smaller groups, varying from four or five individuals to fifty or sixty. In saltwater and brackish areas, tidal fluctuations often trigger movements that can occur at any time of the day. Stormy or windy weather can keep birds moving all day as well.

All divers and sea ducks exhibit dimorphic plumage. The mating, or nuptial, plumage of the males is different and more colorful than that of the drab-colored females. During the summer molt, when they lose all their primary feathers and are flightless for several weeks, the adult drakes lose the colorful nuptial plumage and take on the gray or brown appearance of the females. This "eclipse" plumage is valuable in avoiding predators during the flightless stage.

In the fall, the eclipse plumage of male diving ducks is replaced with a new set of nuptial plumage. By the time most duck seasons open in the lower 48 states, the birds have taken on the colors characteristic of ducks we see on the wintering grounds. In contrast, juvenile male sea ducks exhibit drab eclipse-like plumage for two years. It's not until the second fall after hatching that they exhibit their colorful breeding plumage.

Of the three tribes, the group we refer to as diving ducks (including canvasbacks, redheads, and others) is the most closely related to dabbling ducks. Divers and dabblers share some behavioral traits and often utilize the same habitat. Both are found primarily in freshwater and brackish marshes. Puddle ducks feed in water that is relatively shallow. Most divers feed in water from 1 to 40 feet deep, with ring-necked ducks generally feeding in water less than 6 feet deep, compared to scaup, which regularly feed in water 10–25 feet deep. Compared to puddle ducks, divers sit low in the water. Just before they dive, they compress their body feathers to expel trapped air, which decreases their buoyancy. At times, only a portion of the flock will dive, but often the entire flock will dive at nearly the same moment and then pop up again in quick succession.

Sea ducks, such as this drake common eider, share with diving ducks the behavior of loafing midday between morning and afternoon feeding periods.

Divers consume a combination of plant and animal foods. In general, they consume more animal matter than dabblers do, but the amount of animal matter varies. Redheads feed more on plant material than do other divers, and characteristically 90 percent of their diet is vegetable. In contrast, greater scaup feed primarily on animal material, particularly clams and mussels. The diets of divers can change seasonally, as well. Redheads, for example, consume mostly pondweed and musk grass on their freshwater breeding grounds, then shift their diet to shoal grass on the wintering grounds. In some areas, canvasbacks gorge on water celery during the fall migration, switching to fingernail clams on the wintering areas.

Unlike most dabbling ducks, which nest on land, many diving ducks build a nest of matted vegetation suspended over the water.

Like other diving and sea ducks, these harlequin ducks display dimorphic plumage—that is, the males (left) are more variously patterned and colorful than the females

Some divers do, however, nest on islands or in upland vegetation close to the water's edge. Once the eggs hatch, the hen moves the ducklings to water where there is a higher margin of safety from predators.

Diving ducks nest throughout the broad range of breeding habitats in North America. Species such as canvasbacks, redheads, lesser scaup, and ruddy ducks breed primarily in the Prairie Pothole Region of the north-central United States and the Canadian prairie provinces of Alberta, Saskatchewan, and Manitoba. Here, ice age glaciers scoured the land and left thousands of shallow depressions, or potholes, that seasonally fill with rainwater and snowmelt to form the core breeding habitat for these species. Populations are directly influenced by the amount of wetlands and adjacent upland habitats available. Their fluctuations are closely correlated to the amount of precipitation (snow and rain) in a given year.

While precipitation is vitally important in providing water to the wetland basins, so is a good frost seal. If there is a good frost seal, the ground remains frozen below the surface into the spring, and any precipitation that falls ends up running off into the wetland basins. Conversely, if the frost seal is poor, precipitation percolates into the soil and is lost. In 1999, habitat conditions across the prairies of Canada and the United States were ideal and wetlands were abundant.

The result was one of the highest breeding populations of canvasbacks and redheads in recent years, and the season for both species was open across the nation. By the spring of 2002, dry conditions prevailed and the number of wetland basins plummeted to low levels. The result was a poor hatch of ducks, in general, and canvasbacks, in

Divers and sea ducks require some distance to take off, running along the surface of the water to become airborne.

particular. In 2002–2003, the canvasback season was closed in the United States.

Ring-necked ducks nest primarily in the boreal forest regions of Canada, while greater scaup are tied to their breeding grounds in the tundra regions of Alaska, the Yukon, and the Northwest Territories.

Unlike other divers, greater scaup populations tend to be more stable because they breed in areas that are not as prone to the wet-and-dry cycles common on the prairies.

These areas are not as prone to the wet-and-dry cycles observed in the prairies, and populations of these species tend to be more stable.

The most diverse group, the so-called sea ducks, includes goldeneyes, bufflehead, scoters, eiders, harlequin ducks, long-tailed ducks (oldsquaws), and mergansers. Unlike the diving ducks, sea ducks use their wings to help propel them through the water. As they arch to dive, their wings open and they use their powerful feet to propel themselves to great depths. Long-tailed ducks are the most famous for their deep dives, with birds commonly foraging between 50 and 100 feet below the surface. They have been caught in gill nets in Lake Michigan as deep as 156 feet and in Lake Ontario at 240 feet. Their normal foraging depth is closer to 25 feet, particularly in coastal areas where they feed on mollusks and other invertebrates. Scoters and eiders generally feed in water less than 35 feet deep but are known to forage in deeper water with dives that last more than a minute. Of the sea ducks, goldeneyes, bufflehead, and mergansers forage at depths similar to the diving ducks—usually from 5 to 20 feet. Harlequin ducks utilize stream environments during the breeding season and can be found on nearshore waters, including heavy surf areas, during winter. They are well adapted to these turbulent conditions and shallow waters.

Sea duck food habits also differ from those of most divers. Many species rely heavily on mollusks (including clams and mussels), crustaceans (including crabs and barnacles), other invertebrates, and various aquatic insects. Bufflehead and goldeneyes consume some plant material, particularly pondweed and wild celery, while mergansers subsist almost exclusively on a diet of fish and crustaceans.

Most sea ducks breed in the boreal and tundra regions of North America and are not as prone to the droughts that periodically affect the breeding success of diving and puddle ducks. They choose nest sites along rocky shorelines or near tundra ponds. Some—including the goldeneyes, bufflehead, and hooded mergansers—nest primarily in tree cavities, and in some locales they will nest in man-made nest boxes. Common mergansers use natural cavities and nest boxes, but in some areas show a preference for ground nest sites. Harlequin ducks nest throughout the mountainous regions of northern Rocky Mountains and Pacific Northwest, including Alaska. They prefer nest sites along rocky shores adjacent to the rapids of turbulent streams. Though sea duck breeding habitats tend to be more stable, these species are not as intensively monitored and, consequently, less precise information is available regarding their breeding biology and population levels.

In contrast to dabbling and diving ducks that are capable of breeding the first year after they hatch, sea ducks reach sexual maturity and attain full adult plumage when two years old. For this reason, it can appear that a winter flock of eiders or scoters consists of mostly females, when in reality they include both females and drab-colored first-year males. (A few years ago, for taxidermy, I traveled to Kodiak Island specifically to collect eiders and other sea ducks in their best winter plumage. During the weeklong trip, I spotted several flocks of king eiders and was amazed that only 10 percent of the birds were fully plumed males suitable for mounting. Even though I was likely observing sex ratios equally divided between males and females, only the mature drakes were identifiable.) Females become sexually mature in

Surf scoters in flight.

two years, as well, but their plumage is relatively constant throughout their juvenile and adult stages. Because it takes two years to reach sexual maturity, the breeding potential of sea ducks is lower than that of diving or puddle ducks.

In early fall, adult ducks and their offspring begin to gather in flocks on their staging areas. These birds feed heavily and gain agility on the wing in preparation for their migration to the wintering areas. The migration and its timing are dependent upon both weather patterns and the species. Some species migrate regardless of weather, arriving in certain areas at essentially the same time each year. Scaup migrate south from the boreal forests, arriving at Lake of the Woods on the Ontario-Minnesota border during the second week of October, generally before the first cold front pushes other ducks south. And the first redheads arrive on the Texas Gulf Coast around October 15, when temperatures can be in the high 80s. At other times, the weather, particularly a cold front with freezing rain or snow sweeping out of the north, can push ducks south almost overnight. Some of these mass migrations are spectacular and involve literally millions of waterfowl. If fall weather is mild and cold fronts are absent, however, many birds may linger in Canada and the northern United States, not moving to their wintering grounds until much later than is customary.

These differing migration patterns can work both for and against the hunter. If you know when the birds will arrive at a specific location, you can plan a trip to take advantage of that timing. In the case of weather-dependent migration, a mild fall prolongs the opportunity to effectively hunt ducks if you live in the northern tier of states or Canada. Conversely, if an Alberta Clipper moves though the area early and all the potholes and lakes freeze overnight, your hunting may end sooner than you would like. Hunters on the wintering grounds always hope for an early winter and a cold front that moves birds into their area.

Both biologically and administratively, North America is divided into four flyways—the Pacific, Central, Mississippi, and Atlantic. Waterfowl usually show a greater affinity for a particular flyway than the country as a whole. However, in many instances waterfowl move from one flyway to another in an east-west or west-east direction,

Blaine Burns, Tofield, Alberta
"Understand Duck Migrations"

According to Blaine Burns, an outfitter and former DU biologist, "In areas that stage large numbers of divers during the fall migration, some divers tend to be very traditional in the timing of their stays. In Alberta, canvasbacks stage on Beaverhill Lake. Their numbers increase during the summer, prior to the molt, and build steadily until mid-September. At that time, give or take three or four days, the birds literally move out overnight and the population drops from several thousand to maybe a couple hundred birds. This behavior has been known to occur for many years, and local canvasback hunters know better than to bother hunting them after September 20."

crossing traditional flyway boundaries. For example, some canvasbacks and scaup that breed in prairie region of Canada (which geographically lies in the Central and Mississippi flyways) fly east to wintering grounds on Chesapeake Bay in the Atlantic Flyway. Still, a high percentage of the birds move in a north-south direction, so the flyway concept is useful in managing populations. Redheads that breed in the Prairie Pothole Region of Canada and the United States migrate almost due south to the Gulf Coast of Texas and Mexico, staying within the Central Flyway from start to finish. Other redheads that breed in the Central Flyway fly west to California and the west coast of Mexico in the Pacific Flyway.

The affinity divers and sea ducks have for certain flyways is particularly evident on the wintering grounds. Harvest data is a good indicator of these tendencies. Redheads, for example, winter primarily in the Central and Mississippi flyways where the harvest is almost equally divided. The combined harvest of redheads in these flyways represents 75 percent of the total United States harvest (1965 to 2001 averages). The Pacific Flyway accounted for 20 percent, and the Atlantic only 5 percent. Scaup show a preference for the Mississippi Flyway, where 61 percent of the harvest occurs, followed by 17 percent in the Central, 14 percent in the Atlantic, and 8 percent in the Pacific. Ruddy ducks have a more even distribution of harvest, with 38 percent bagged in the Pacific Flyway, 32 in the Mississippi, 17 in the Atlantic, and 13 percent in the Central. Sea ducks have the most extreme derivation of harvest. About 90 percent of the long-tailed ducks are taken in the Atlantic Flyway, as are 80 to 85 percent of the three species of scoters, while 78 percent of the harlequin ducks are bagged in the Pacific Flyway, the majority of those in Alaska.

Within each flyway there are traditional wintering areas for certain species of divers and sea ducks, as well as a combination of species. Traditional wintering grounds in the Pacific Flyway include Kodiak

Island, where a variety of sea ducks are found, including harlequins, long-tailed ducks, greater scaup, goldeneyes, scoters, and a few king and common eiders. The Puget Sound region in Washington is also a melting pot for sea ducks and divers, with scoters, harlequins, goldeneyes, and scaup all present. In winter, San Francisco Bay hosts impressive canvasback populations along with scaup and surf scoters. Inland, Utah's Bear River marshes support good populations of canvasbacks and redheads during migration, while some redheads and scaup continue south into Mexico. In the Central Flyway, Freezeout Lake, Montana, hosts a variety of diving ducks during migration. About 85 percent of the continental population of redheads winter in coastal Texas and northeastern Mexico. Long Point, Ontario, in the Mississippi Flyway, is an important migration area for canvasbacks, ring-necked ducks, redheads, and scaup, while the Upper Mississippi River on the Wisconsin-Iowa border hosts more canvasbacks in November than any other single location in the United States. Farther south, Catahoula Lake in Louisiana supports impressive numbers of canvasbacks and ringed-necked ducks. On the Atlantic Flyway, the coast of Maine is a primary wintering area for common eiders, while Chesapeake Bay provides winter habitat for canvasbacks, scaup, scoters, and long-tailed ducks. In North Carolina, the Pamlico and Currituck sounds are important wintering areas for all three species of scoters.

While these areas are traditional migration and wintering areas, ducks—being the mobile creatures they are—can literally pick up and move overnight. Migration areas can be great examples of the old adage "You should have been here yesterday." Ducks respond to their own built-in time clock, weather, local food resources, hunting pressure, and other factors that make them less predictable, particularly during migration periods. On the wintering grounds, where conditions are generally more stable, sea ducks and divers have a tendency to use the same areas and be more predictable than puddle ducks, which are notorious for moving from one region to another within a given wintering area.

Unlike dabblers, which often move in relation to the discovery of a new food resource and can descend on a newly harvested cornfield or flooded rice field like locust, divers rely on aquatic vegetation and animal foods that generally don't change their location. That's not to say divers won't capitalize on new food resources or move to new areas. Several years ago the Sacramento River reached flood stage and overflowed into many regions of California's Central Valley. Some of these overflow areas were previously harvested rice fields. Canvasbacks, presumably from the San Francisco Bay area, somehow found this new food resource, and thousands of birds flocked to the flooded grain.

Once divers and sea ducks reach the wintering grounds, they use the abundant food resources to maintain body condition for the all-important breeding season ahead. Courtship in some species begins as early as December, while the birds are still on the wintering grounds, and continues throughout the spring, with the final frenzied activity on the breeding grounds. The courtship activity of most divers and sea ducks takes place while swimming, in contrast to the aerial courtship displays of many puddle ducks. Familiar courtship activity includes the head-throw ritual of goldeneyes, the neck inflation and cooing of redheads, and the head-bobbing of ruddy ducks. Once a pair bond is formed, it is maintained throughout the winter and spring. The males stay with the females until incubation begins, at which time the males leave the females and the pair bond dissolves.

Diving and sea ducks take the prize when it comes to being hardy. Compared to blue-winged teal that migrate south before there's even the slightest hint of cold weather, species such as goldeneyes stay in the northern areas as long as there is open water. But no species of waterfowl can compare to the hardiness of eiders. They winter in areas where other ducks only stop briefly, and they spend the coldest days of the year in salt water where ambient temperatures often drop to below zero. The wintering grounds of the spectacled eider were unknown until the mid-1990s, when an aerial survey in the Bering Sea found a massive flock in the middle of pack ice several hundred miles offshore. The eiders were maintaining open water in the ice via their body heat and movement alone. Eiders are able to winter in such harsh environments because their animal-food diet provides continuous nourishment, and their heavy layer of protective down provides excellent insulation.

Divers and sea ducks have occupied North American habitats for centuries, withstanding the rigors of long-distance migrations, drought, floods, severe weather, predators, and a host of other challenges that Mother Nature throws at them. They have responded with amazing resilience, yet their future is not secure, primarily because of the loss of wetland habitats on the breeding grounds, as well as habitat loss in migration areas and on the wintering grounds. These are the result of changes to the environment by humans, not acts of nature. Only we have the ability to prevent the destruction of wetland habitats. If it is our goal to have waterfowl for future generations, the lakes, marshes, potholes, oxbow lakes, saltwater estuaries, and rocky coastlines upon which they depend must be preserved and restored. If done properly, our grandchildren can witness the spectacle of migration, huddle in an offshore blind as a flock of canvasbacks blasts through the decoys, or watch a brood of redheads play follow the leader in a prairie wetland. The future is ours to decide.

History of Diver and Sea Duck Hunting

European cave paintings thousands of years old depict waterfowl; paintings in ancient Egyptian tombs portray pharaohs hunting ducks with bow and arrow. In North American, hunting for ducks has likely occurred since the first Native Americans crossed the Bering land

© Edward J. Moxley

A sporting gentleman from the latter part of the nineteenth century with a bag of diving ducks and a fine double gun.

bridge and took up residence in the New World. Further evidence of man's desire to hunt ducks was discovered in 1924 near the Stillwater Marshes of Nevada, where a basket containing eleven canvasback decoys made of reeds and animal skins was discovered. Carbon dating indicated the decoys were nearly two thousand years old. Accounts of the early explorers include tales of American Indians capturing flightless waterfowl by hand or herding them into makeshift traps. It wasn't until white settlers from Europe came to the New World with their muskets that duck hunting changed dramatically. The hunting was still for food, but the introduction of firearms increased hunting success markedly. As settlers moved from the eastern seaboard to the interior of the country, accounts of waterfowl that blackened the skies and terms like "great clouds of ducks" came from the Grand Prairie of Arkansas, the lower Mississippi River Valley, the Dakotas, the Great Lakes, the Gulf Coast, and eventually the Platte River Bottoms, Great Salt Lake, and other vast marshes of the West.

Throughout the 1700s and into the early 1800s, duck hunting served one purpose—to put food on the table. A few ducks were killed and sold and a few were bartered for hard goods like flour and sugar, but it wasn't until the mid-1800s that market hunting began in earnest. It was during this period that hunting for ducks became serious business. Soon, the canvasback became one of the most highly desired species, and hundreds of barrels of them made their way from Chesapeake Bay to the major cities along the Atlantic seaboard. A canvasback dinner might set you back two dollars in New York or Philadelphia, and a redhead from the Gulf Coast might be the duck du jour in a New Orleans hotel dining room.

Sport hunting of ducks came into its own during the same period. The hunting was for the table, not the marketplace. While a daily bag could be large, it was meager compared to the hundreds of ducks a market hunter might kill and sell in a day. Because many of the population centers were on the East Coast, duck hunting, particularly for divers, first came into vogue there. Chesapeake Bay's legendary canvasback and scaup shooting attracted hunters from Washington, D.C. and Baltimore, and the bluebills, black ducks, and brant of Barnegat

Bay brought hunters from Philadelphia and Newark. The Great Lakes region offered gunning for divers; famous venues included the marshes of Long Point, Ontario, and Lake St. Clair near Detroit. In the Mississippi Delta, hunters concentrated their efforts on the canvasbacks that wintered in Mobile Bay, while redheads were the targets along the coast of Texas near Houston. For San Francisco Bay area residents, the open water of the bay and marshes in the Sacramento-San Joaquin Delta provided shooting for canvasbacks and scaup close to home.

The first duck clubs were founded on the Atlantic Coast as early as 1861. Among the earliest were the Corwin Gunning Camp on Long Island and the Cobb Island Club on Virginia's Eastern Shore. Later, more waterfowl hunting clubs were established in prime waterfowl migration and wintering areas across the country. Club members were generally businessmen who found a weekend at the duck club a welcome respite from city life. Market hunters used both live and wooden decoys, and it wasn't long before sport hunters began using wooden decoys as their primary method of attracting ducks. The canvasback and bluebill rigs of that era were impressive, often numbering in the hundreds. These decoys were made one at a time by master carvers. Eventually commercial operations began mass-producing decoys to meet the growing demand. Duck calling originated as an effective way to attract puddle ducks, particularly mallards. Divers also respond to calls, but most of the early diver calling was done by mouth or with mallard calls.

By the late 1800s, the seemingly endless supply of waterfowl began to decline due, in part, to the relentless shooting by both sport and market hunters. Even more disturbing was the expansion of agricultural activity into prime waterfowl breeding and staging areas. The rate of agricultural expansion and wetland drainage was particularly alarming in the Prairie Pothole Region of the north-central United States and south-central Canada. Homesteaders flocked to this previously unsettled expanse to lay claim to land and scratch out an existence by farm-ing. By the early 1900s, mechanized equipment replaced horse-drawn implements, and wetland drainage was accelerated. Within a decade, steam-driven draglines—and the proliferation of the drainage ditches they produced—had an adverse impact on waterfowl habitat and pop-ulations across the landscape.

More hunters and fewer birds prompted the promulgation of new regulations to preserve waterfowl. The first was the Migratory Bird Treaty Act of 1913, signed by the United States and Great Britain for the protection of birds moving seasonally between Canada and the United States. It placed regulatory and management activities for migratory birds under federal control. The first federal hunting regula-tions were established in 1918. They included a 100-day season and a limit of 25 ducks and 8 geese daily. That same year, the U.S. Bureau of Biological Survey (later to become the U.S. Fish and Wildlife Service) was established. In 1936, the Migratory Bird Treaty was signed by the United States and Mexico. The 1913 and 1936 treaties continue to provide the basis for the international management of waterfowl in North America.

It was during the U.S. Bureau of Biological Survey's early years that the concept of banding, or "ringing" as it is known in Europe, began. It soon became the primary tool in determining waterfowl migration patterns and later contributed to the setting of harvest regu-lations. Band recovery data was also instrumental in determining the location of several national wildlife refuges. Undoubtedly, banding data's most significant value was the designation of the four major fly-ways and the establishment of the flyway-management system. Today, we know that waterfowl management extends well beyond the concept of the four flyways, but its establishment paved the way for manage-ment in a systematic fashion.

Biologists have determined that the number of ducks varies from year to year and decade to decade. Their populations are largely dependent on natural conditions, particularly wet-and-dry climatic cycles. Ducks are generally able to cope with these highs and lows, but none of the lows in recent history can compare to the Dust Bowl days of the 1930s. Everything suffered—people, livestock, crops, and wildlife. Duck seasons were as short as 16 days, limits as low as 3 birds daily, and canvasback and redhead seasons were closed. The most important waterfowl breeding area—the Prairie Pothole Region of the United States and Canada—was the hardest hit, and the farmlands and wetlands yielded neither crops nor ducks. Waterfowl numbers dwindled to the lowest level in recorded history. It became evident that laws, treaties, and regulations could not alone conserve waterfowl.

The Dust Bowl rallied conservationists and the government, instituting management and acquisition efforts to reverse the tide of the waterfowl decline. Due to the efforts of men like Teddy Roosevelt, as early as 1903, the federal government had managed to acquire about 750,000 acres of habitat for wildlife conservation. By the early 1940s, some three million acres had been set aside, much of it for the preservation of waterfowl. Many of these new lands were purchased using monies generated by the Migratory Bird Hunting Stamp Act of 1934, which required all hunters age sixteen and older to purchase a duck stamp to legally hunt waterfowl. The $1 stamp immediately generated millions of dollars that were used for the acquisition of waterfowl habitat. Today, the same stamp costs $15, and the majority of the proceeds still go directly to habitat acquisition.

In 1937, the Pittman-Robertson Act was passed by Congress authorizing an 11 percent excise tax on the sale of sporting firearms and ammunition. These funds were collected by the federal government and allocated to state fish and game agencies for wildlife management purposes. Since 1937, hundreds of millions of dollars have been allocated to all fifty states for wildlife conservation purposes, including many projects specifically for waterfowl.

In 1937, Ducks Unlimited was founded by concerned hunters who believed that money could be raised to preserve and manage wetland habitats for the benefit of waterfowl. Since then, DU has raised more than $1.6 billion for waterfowl conservation in Canada, the United States, and Mexico. Those dollars have conserved some 10 million acres of habitat, from the Canadian tundra to the tropics of Mexico.

It was also during the 1930s that the modern method of surveying waterfowl breeding grounds began. Today this greatly expanded effort involves the coordination of biologists in the United States and Canada traveling census routes in aircraft, vehicles, and boats to determine the status of waterfowl breeding populations. The same routes are traveled every year in May and again in July in order to predict the size of the fall flight. This data is an integral part of the information used to establish annual waterfowl hunting regulations. In addition to the breeding ground surveys, winter inventories add another dimension to the census data.

Since the 1940s, waterfowl populations have fluctuated, largely due to periodic droughts and wet periods that naturally occur. Below-normal rainfall and snowpack in the 1950s triggered a severe drought. Regulations that had slowly been liberalized after the Dust Bowl once again became restrictive. In the 1970s, the point system was established in some flyways. Depending on the species, using the point system up to 10 ducks per person could be harvested daily. In the 1980s, again due to drought, the point system was abolished and limits were reduced. By the mid-1990s, populations rebounded as wet cycles returned. In 1999, the number of waterfowl counted on the breeding ground was the highest since the surveys began, and the fall flight forecast was more than 100 million ducks for the first time in history. Liberal regulations went into effect in all flyways across the nation, with seasons as long as 107 days, limits as high as 7 ducks daily, and canvasbacks were legal to shoot. In the boom-and-bust world of ducks, breeding ground conditions deteriorated in 2002 and duck hunting regulations in some states became more restrictive than in 2001. For the first time in many years, the canvasback season was closed in the United States. Throughout these wet-and-dry cycles, and resulting roller coaster duck populations, one factor was constant: the loss of wetlands. The rate of loss has slowed significantly in recent years, but losses continue to occur every day.

Modern wildlife management still hasn't found a way to stop the decrease in waterfowl numbers that occur when Mother Nature fails to deliver enough moisture to the prairies. However, modern technology—including satellite imagery, computer modeling, and radio telemetry—is helping biologists and researchers gather more-accurate data to manage our precious waterfowl heritage. We as citizens can do our part by supporting organizations like Ducks Unlimited and lobbying our elected representatives to support conservation efforts and supply funds to implement them. We must work as a team to help waterfowl through the tough times, and share in the bounty when appropriate.

Diver and Sea Duck Hunting Today

Since the first waterfowlers carved decoys and launched their wooden boats, the pursuit of diving and sea ducks has been a sport rich in tradition, practiced by a relatively small but dedicated group of hunters. These hunters keep track of the tides and weather; learn the habits and migration patterns of the birds; make or acquire large decoy spreads; maintain boats, motors, and blinds; and endure cold, wet, and occasionally treacherous weather for the sole purpose of pursuing big-water ducks. The reward for all their effort has been uncrowded hunting areas, the smell of salt air and the feel of a Nor'easter building, or the sight of a flock of bluebills or canvasbacks coming full-tilt into their decoys.

A diver hunter takes a drake redhead from his Chesapeake Bay retriever on the Laguna Madre in Texas.

Atlantic Coast gunning venues today stretch from the rocky shores of Nova Scotia and Maine, where hunters seek eiders from half-tide ledges; to Chesapeake Bay, where canvasbacks and scaup come to off-shore blinds; to the Carolinas, where scoters are gunned from boat blinds. The Upper Mississippi River is known for canvasbacks, while Catahoula Lake in Louisiana attracts hunters who hold canvasbacks and ringnecks in high esteem. If redheads are your quarry, then the Gulf Coast of Texas and Mexico provides memorable action.

Along Pacific shores, diver and sea duck hunting is popular from Kodiak Island in the north, where exotic species including harlequins, long-tailed ducks, and king eiders spend the winter, to Washington, where goldeneyes and scoters are hunted from floating blinds in Puget Sound. Farther south, California's San Francisco Bay hosts an impressive assemblage of canvasbacks, scaup, and scoters that are hunted from blinds that have been used for more than 100 years. While big-water duck hunting areas are abundant and varied, hunters must find their own locations and choose their own hunting methods and equipment, whether it be a guided or do-it-yourself excursion.

While many areas are well known for their diver and sea duck hunting, other less-chronicled areas also provide solid action. National wildlife refuges and state wildlife areas, many set aside specifically for waterfowl, provide waterfowl hunting opportunities throughout the country. Puddle ducks or geese are the species most frequently bagged, but the enterprising hunter who expends the effort can often locate areas where divers and sea ducks concentrate.

Several years ago, while hunting puddle ducks on a state wildlife area in Nevada, I noticed flight after flight of redheads and scaup flying well out of range and then dropping into a distant marsh. At first I thought it was in a closed zone, but after my partners and I finished hunting we decided to check it out anyway. Eventually, we reached what we thought was the area—a series of ponds that were completely surrounded by tall bulrush. The bulrush was so tall and thick that we could not see through or over it from the roadway. To get a better look we crawled on top of my camper. Standing on the roof we could see open water and were astounded to see at least 500 redheads and scaup, plus a few dozen canvasbacks and ring-necked ducks. The ducks were out of sight of every vehicle that passed by, and best of all, the area was open to hunting.

The next day we arrived in the dark, grabbed two bags of decoys, and busted through 50 yards of bulrush to get to the open water. After considerable effort, we finally stood at the edge of the bulrush in two feet of water and set out the decoys. For the next two hours redheads, scaup, cans, and ringnecks literally poured into the pond, and the action was fast and furious. We had our canvasback and redhead limits of one bird each in no time, and we then filled out the limit of seven birds with bluebills and ringnecks. When we showed our birds to the attendant at the hunter check station, even he was surprised. Not every hunch turns out this well, but the moral of the story is to not be afraid

Hunting diving and sea ducks often requires extra effort—like the setting out of large decoy spreads—but many waterfowlers find the rewards of hunting uncrowded areas well worth it.

of public areas, always investigate interesting sightings, and follow up on tips from other hunters or wildlife department employees.

While areas specifically set aside for waterfowl by federal and state agencies provide more habitat for puddle ducks and geese than they do divers or sea ducks, the big-water duck hunter still has several advantages. Lakes, large rivers, coastal lagoons, bays, and offshore areas that divers and sea ducks frequent are often considered navigable waterways and are open to hunting. As a result, they become de facto public hunting areas. Unlike other state and federal areas that often control access and hunter numbers, hunting opportunities can be wide open. The public hunting areas can get crowded, but big-water areas see few hunters. The reason is simple: Hunting divers and sea ducks requires more gear and planning—boats and outboards, large decoy spreads, a launch site, and so forth. Not everyone is willing to make the effort. In contrast, hip boots and a handful of decoys are often all that's needed to successfully hunt puddle ducks. In my book, the ability to hunt uncrowded areas is worth the extra effort.

The topic of hunting pressure brings up the subject of hunter ethics. In a country that thrives on competition, some hunters look at duck hunting with the same competitive spirit. Often the most aggressive competitor is also the most successful, but this "attitude" can lead to poor behavior in the field. It's every hunter's duty to conduct himself responsibly. This means obeying the laws and regulations and considering the rights of other hunters.

One of the most questionable behaviors I see in the field is hunters shooting at birds that are out of range, commonly referred to as "sky busting" or "sky scraping." Shooting at ducks out of range can cripple ducks that die later, conditions ducks to fly higher, and ruins the experience for others who patiently wait for the birds to decoy. Although it can be difficult to determine the right shooting distance, if you pay attention to the distance at which you consistently kill birds and spend time on the sporting clays range (concentrating on target distance), you'll find sky scraping declines or disappears.

By reducing sky scraping, a significant number of ducks that would otherwise be crippled and lost will be conserved. Another effective conservation measure is the use of a trained retriever. Not only does a dog reduce the number of birds lost, watching a well-trained retriever is one of the joys of duck hunting. A dog also reduces the amount of hard work you have to do. Instead of taking the time to untie the boat to pick up dead birds, you can simply send the dog to retrieve while keeping the boat anchored. Not everyone has the time to train a dog or the space to house one, but for those who do, a good dog is a valuable asset. Equally as valuable— and certainly less expensive—is having a hunting partner with a good retriever.

Make no bones about it, a well-trained retriever enhances the duck hunting experience in many ways.

In a world where the anti-hunting interests are looking for any situation they can exploit, we don't need to provide them with real-life stories of bad behavior and game law violations. We certainly don't want to perpetuate the Elmer Fudd image that many uninformed people have of hunters. It is our duty to keep our own house clean if we are to maintain our sport into the future.

Perhaps the most important factor in the future of duck hunting is the introduction of youngsters to the sport. Kids have plenty of diversions to occupy their spare time in today's world of video games, boom boxes, and TV. But if each of us takes the time to invite one youth to hunt waterfowl with us each season, the chances of them getting hooked on hunting is far greater than if they sit at home watching TV. Taking a kid hunting is now easier than ever with the advent of junior waterfowl hunts and other special youth hunts. If only a few of the kids introduced to waterfowling become active waterfowl hunters as adults, it will help maintain our hunting heritage into the future.

Since my first day hunting divers on San Pablo Bay, I have had the good fortune to meet and hunt with a variety of individuals, including long-time hunting buddies, casual acquaintances, and full-time hunting guides. Like most other hunters, I have seen red-hot action and I've sat in a blind all day without firing a shot. Both the successes and failures have taught me to be a better hunter. I have met people that shared the same passion I have for duck hunting and have learned from them. Each time I launch the boat in a new location and feel the cold air in my face, it is both the chance for a rewarding experience and an opportunity to learn more about the sport. I'm glad that duck hunting—and specifically gunning for divers and sea ducks—occupies an important part of my hunting year.

TOP TEN DIVER AND SEA DUCK HUNTING DESTINATIONS

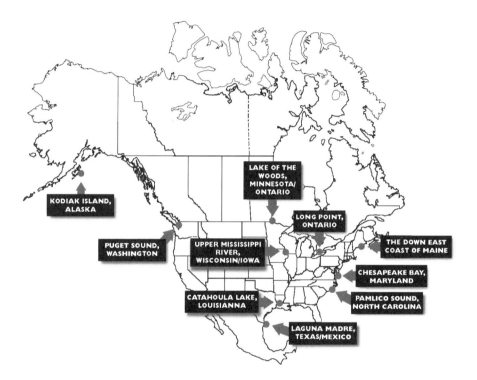

T hroughout North America there are dozens of outstanding locations to hunt for divers and sea ducks. They range from Canadian prairie potholes to the coastlines of the Atlantic and Pacific to the lagunas of Mexico and many places in between. Many of them are well known; some are not known at all. In preparation for this book, I spent the past several waterfowl seasons traveling around North America, experiencing firsthand the diver and sea duck hunting in a dozen different locations in Canada, the United States, and Mexico. Based on these visits, other trips, and research, I have come up with what I, along with many waterfowl biologists and avid duck hunters, consider the top ten diving and sea duck hunting destinations in North America. The destinations are presented not in order of preference but from north to south, following the migration from the breeding grounds to the migration areas and finally to the wintering grounds.

Lake of the Woods is famous for its fine bluebill hunting.

Lake of the Woods, Minnesota and Ontario

Lake of the Woods is a million-acre chunk of north woods real estate in northern Minnesota, western Ontario, and southeastern Manitoba. Carved by glaciers, its rocky granite islands, secluded bays, and wild rice beds provide habitat for nesting waterfowl—primarily puddle ducks, along with common goldeneyes, ring-necked ducks, bufflehead, and common mergansers. Additionally, the area is a major migration stopover for ducks heading south, particularly divers. The lake is 65 miles long and up to 55 miles wide, with more than 65,000 miles of shoreline and 14,582 islands.

Puddle duck hunting is best early in the season, while the best diver shooting is generally in October. This region is an important staging area for bluebills, with the first birds showing up in early October. They stop to feed and rest on their way south, with good populations present until late October or early November. Other divers— including bufflehead, goldeneyes, ring-necked ducks, and a few redheads and canvasbacks—also show up in October. Divers continue funneling though until early to mid-November,

Many waterfowlers hunt Lake of the Woods on their own, bringing their own boats, decoy sets, and—yes—a trusty retriever.

when the area ices up and the last birds head south. The season in Ontario generally opens in mid-September and closes in December, while the Minnesota season opens in late September or early October and closes in December.

Most of the hunting occurs from points, where hunters use makeshift driftwood or rock blinds for concealment and large decoy spreads bring the birds in close. As long as you don't hunt near areas of human habitation, the shoreline and waters of the lake are open to hunting. Other hunters use boat blinds anchored in local flyways. When the birds are "in," hunters clean up on scaup, which account for about 70 percent of the diving duck bag on Lake of the Woods. Many hunters come to Lake of the Woods to hunt ducks on their own. They have boats and large decoy sets and have learned how to hunt the huge lake. If you hunt on your own, it's important to spend time scouting and make sure you get a map of the lake—with hundreds of coves and waterways it's easy to get lost. Also, know that a sudden wind can whip calm water into a raging torrent in a matter of minutes, so always be safety conscious.

Because Lake of the Wood straddles the United States–Canada border, it's possible to hunt in Ontario, shoot a limit of ducks, and cross back into Minnesota to shoot a second limit the same day. This is perfectly legal, provided you possess both Ontario and Minnesota hunting licenses and the required migratory bird hunting stamps, abide by the possession limits, and make legal border crossings.

Lake of the Woods can be accessed from Warroad and Zipple Bay on the Minnesota side and Kenora and Morson in Ontario. However, some of the best hunting on the Minnesota side is accessed via the Northwest Angle. The Angle is surrounded on three sides by Canada but belongs to the United States due to a mapping error. It seems that in defining the boundary between Canada and the United States after the French and Indian War, a mistake was made and the United States ended up owning title to land that logically should belong to Canada. Access is via Sprague, Manitoba, into Canada and then back into Minnesota on Highways 308 and 525 to Young's Bay. There are stores and accommodations at Young's Bay that are open year-round, as well as resorts on Oak and Flagg Islands. Boat passenger service to Oak and Flagg Islands can be arranged by the resorts.

In addition to do-it-yourself trips, a few of the Minnesota resorts offer guided hunts. Frank Walsh operates Walsh's Bay Store Camp (800-214-2533; www.baystorecamp.com) on Oak Island. He's been offering guided waterfowl packages for ten years and has several guides at his disposal. Many his guides are also fishing guides during the summer who know the massive lake like their own backyards. Bay Store Camp offers a four-night/three-day hunting package that includes accommodations in individual cabins, boat with motor, and guide service (double occupancy, two to a boat/guide). The boats are 18-footers that can handle the big water. He also offers lodging and boat packages for do-it-yourself hunters.

Additionally, Angle Inn Lodge (800-879-4986; www.angleinnlodge.com), also on Oak Island, offers accommodations, meals, and boats for hunters who have decoys and hunt on their own.

For general information contact the Minnesota DNR (218-755-3955; www.dnr.state.mn.us) or Ontario Ministry of Natural Resources (800-667-1940 or 416-314-2000; www.mnr.gov.on.ca/MNR).

Long Point, Ontario

Less than a mile wide along much of its length, Long Point stretches about 20 miles into Lake Erie. Long Point Bay and its associated marshes form one of the most important waterfowl staging areas in North America, particularly for scaup and canvasbacks, along with lesser numbers of redheads and ring-necked ducks. The marshes and bay provide an abundance of submerged aquatic vegetation, including musk grass and wild celery. Along with zebra mussels, they provide the primary food resources for migrating diving ducks. The area is used both spring and fall, hosting diving duck populations that have exceeded 100,000 birds.

While a few puddle ducks nest on Long Point, it is in early October that the first waves of divers reach the area. Ring-necked ducks and scaup are the first to arrive, followed by canvasbacks and redheads. Peak populations of all species of divers are present from early November to early December. By mid-December, the marshes and near-shore waters are generally iced-over, forcing the birds south. In recent years some diving ducks have stayed on until late December and provided good shooting. The season in Ontario usually opens in late September and closes in late December.

Waterfowlers must purchase a special permit to hunt in either of Long Point's two zones.

Long Point is a unique combination of public and private lands that have been protected from large-scale development. In 1866, the Long Point Company purchased the majority of the peninsula and established a private duck club that is still in operation today. Later, the Long Point Waterfowl Management Unit was established by the provincial government. The waterfowl unit is divided into two hunting zones. In Zone A, hunters with reservations and first-come, first-served hunters are admitted on Mondays, Wednesdays, Fridays, and Saturdays during the waterfowl season. Reservation applications can be mailed to the Long Point Waterfowl Unit (P.O. Box 99, Port Rowan, Ontario N0E 1M0) at least 15 days prior to the date you would like to hunt. Applications are accepted on forms available from the waterfowl unit, or just send a postcard that contains your name, address, and the date you wish to hunt. If you are selected, a $12 fee is payable upon entry. Hunters are required to check in and out of the area at the provincial park, and there are a maximum number of hunters (variable by year) allowed on the area at any one time. Within Zone A, all hunters are either assigned a blind in the marsh portion of the zone or a stake in the outer hunting zone. A stake is a location where a layout boat or boat blind can be anchored. For diver hunters, the stakes are the most productive areas.

Zone B is a large area where hunters can buy an annual permit ($25) and hunt anywhere within the zone. Hunters are not required to check in but must report the number and species of birds harvested. In Zone B there are some stands of emergent vegetation, but a good percentage of the hunting is done from anchored and layout boats.

In addition to the public hunting area, open-water hunting is permitted six days per week (no Sunday hunting in Ontario). Within the Inner Bay there are both designated hunting and sanctuary zones, so be sure you know where you are hunting and obey all signs. Some of the best areas for open-water hunting in the Inner Bay are Turkey Point, Big and Little Rice bays, and Thoroughfare Point. Outer Bay open-water hunting is unrestricted. Look for rafts of divers or flight paths and set up accordingly. Bluebill decoys (60–120) are the choice of the locals, with a few canvasback or redhead blocks thrown in for good measure. One of the most popular and productive open-water hunting methods at Long Point is layout boat gunning. And with one of North America's most respected layout boat builders (Bankes Boats, www.banksboats.com) based near Long Point, it's no wonder.

In addition to hunting the public wildlife management area and open-water areas on your own, there are several guides that operate in Long Point Bay. Among them are Blind Expectations, a guide service

Layout boat gunning is one of the most productive methods for hunting divers in open water on any one of Long Point's numerous bays.

owned and operated by Emile Vandommele (519-586-7560; vandommele@kwic.com). He has been operating in the Long Point area for ten years, hunting divers and dabblers from camouflaged boats and layout rigs surrounded by large decoy spreads. He offers day hunts that include accommodations in Port Rowan.

Another operation is Coletta Bay Guides (727-546-7517 winter/spring, 519-586-7203 summer/fall) owned and operated by Don Millar. Millar has offered shoreline, boat blind, layout boat, and sneak boat gunning for both puddle ducks and divers for thirty years. He offers day hunts and can provide accommodations.

For more information contact the Ontario Ministry of Natural Resources (800-667-1940 or 416-314-2000; www.mnr.gov.on.ca/MNR).

Upper Mississippi River, Wisconsin and Iowa

In the Mississippi Flyway, the series of dams and locks in the Upper Mississippi River are an important staging and migration area for canvasbacks, scaup, goldeneyes, and bufflehead. The section of river most important to waterfowl extends from Winona, Minnesota, to Dubuque, Iowa, and it is part of the Upper Mississippi River National Wildlife and Fish Refuge. The section covers 145 river miles, is a navigable waterway, and is open to hunting. There are, however, some designated no-hunting zones within this stretch. While diving ducks use the entire river corridor, the primary staging areas for canvasbacks and other divers are Pools 7, 8, and 9 near La Crosse, Wisconsin.

Canvasbacks and other divers begin arriving in mid-October, with huntable numbers generally present by late October. The divers stay until ice forces them to move to their primary wintering areas on Chesapeake Bay in Maryland and Catahoula Lake in Louisiana. At the peak of the migration, more than 300,000 canvasbacks and 80,000 scaup have been counted on Pool 9 alone. In most years, the river is frozen by Thanksgiving or early December, with only a few hardy goldeneyes and common mergansers remaining to spend the winter.

Big boats and big decoy spreads are needed to hunt the big waters of the Upper Mississippi River.

While there is some shore-based hunting, most divers here are gunned from anchored boats. The boats vary in size from 12 to more than 20 feet in length and are covered with camouflage material of some type. Much of the hunting occurs on the Wisconsin side of the

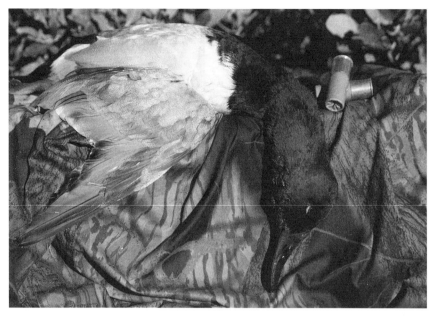

When the canvasback season is open, taking a prized can from the Upper Mississippi River can be the icing on the cake of a fine day of diver hunting.

river. Wisconsin law requires that the boat be anchored within 100 feet of the shoreline or in emergent vegetation that provides at least partial concealment. This effectively prevents boats from being anchored in open water. While the locations change from year to year, there is always enough emergent vegetation to provide hunters numerous spots to choose from. As you might expect, there are several favored locations that seem to be used by hunters on most days. There are numerous boat launching ramps on both the Iowa and Wisconsin sides. Most hunters use massive decoy spreads, often up to 200, to lure the birds from the huge rafts of ducks that are visible in the open water of the river.

Hunters looking for a guide can contact Tony Toye of Big River Guide Service (608-375-7447; toyedecoys@tds.net). Toye is a Coast Guard–licensed small-boat captain and has been guiding full time on the Mississippi River for seven years. He specializes in mallards and canvasbacks, but his clients have harvested up to twenty species of ducks. Hunting is from 18- and 20-foot boat blinds that are covered with reeds, surrounded by 150 decoys, and anchored in local flyways. The boat blinds can accommodate up to four hunters and the guide. While Toye does not provide accommodations, he recommends the Picatee Creek Lodge (608-874-4187; www.picateecreeklodge.com), a large furnished cabin with a full kitchen that can handle up to six hunters.

The season is generally from early October to early December. In 2002–2003, the canvasback season was closed throughout the United States. For additional information, contact the Iowa DNR (515-281-5918 or 515-281-4687; www.iowadnr.com) or the Wisconsin DNR (608-266-2621; www.dnr.state.wi.us), Upper Mississippi River Refuge, La Crosse District, Pools 7 and 8 (608-783-8405) and McGregor District, Pools 9, 10, and 11 (563-873-3423).

These harlequin ducks are just one of the many species of sea ducks found on Kodiak Island.

Kodiak Island, Alaska

Sea duck hunting has long been a popular sport on the Atlantic Coast, but on the West Coast it has never really taken hold. One notable exception is Kodiak Island. In the past decade, the demand for sea duck hunting, particularly by individuals interested in adding certain species to their taxidermy collections, has increased significantly. Despite its far north location, Kodiak Island is primarily a wintering area. Some breeding does occur and certain species of ducks pass through the area on their way south, but Kodiak has gained popularity among hunters as a prime location for sea ducks. The island is roughly 100 miles long and 50 miles wide, located about an hour's flight from Anchorage in the Gulf of Alaska.

Beginning in September, several species of puddle ducks leave their northern breeding areas in Alaska and Canada and migrate to Kodiak, where they pause to feed and rest on their southward journey. By October, these birds are joined by diving and sea ducks that have left the bitter cold of the Arctic for milder conditions. Many continue south along the Pacific Flyway and end up in Washington, Oregon, and California.

Due to its maritime climate, Kodiak's weather is moderate by Alaska standards. While winter can be damp and cold, the bays and estuaries seldom freeze. Add waters rich in plankton and invertebrates and Kodiak has evolved as

Kodiak Island is one of the few places where waterfowlers can hunt the majestic king eider.

an important wintering area for scoters (white-winged, surf, black), goldeneyes (common and Barrow's), long-tailed ducks, harlequins, bufflehead, and red-breasted mergansers. And while their numbers are relatively low, it is the most southerly wintering grounds for king, common (Pacific subspecies), and Steller's eiders. In fact, many eiders are not forced south until December when pack ice forms in the Bering Sea. Eiders, both king and Pacific, are the biggest challenge of any trip to Kodiak. The population of these birds varies from year to year, with the most severe winters forcing the largest number of eiders south to Kodiak. Also, be aware that the protected Steller's eider is found on Kodiak and often decoys better than the other eiders. The protected emperor goose is occasionally seen, as well, so be sure of your target.

The season is generally early October to late January. For years there has been a special limit of 10 sea ducks per day, 20 in possession, which could be taken in addition to a general limit of diving and puddle ducks. For Alaska residents, these dual limits remain unchanged. However, a law implemented in 1999 requires nonresidents to include sea ducks as part of their general limits, which on Kodiak is typically 7 ducks daily and 21 in possession. Further, nonresidents can take no more than 20 sea ducks total for the season, to include no more than 4 king eiders, Pacific (common) eiders, harlequins, long-tailed ducks (oldsquaws), black scoters, white-winged scoters, or surf scoters each. No special regulations apply to nonresidents when hunting puddle and diving ducks. While puddle ducks are hunted early in the season and good populations of diving and sea ducks are present beginning in November, serious hunting for sea ducks does not occur until December and January, when their plumage is prime.

Most hunting is from the offshore islands and rocks, where little more than good camouflage clothing and a few rocks or driftwood logs stacked up on a point act as a blind. A set of decoys that mimics the target species works best, but a mixed set of scoter and goldeneye decoys seems to be the best combination to attract the greatest variety of species.

I should also point out that some of the hunting on Kodiak is not traditional ducks over decoys. While a good percentage of your time will be spent hunting over decoys—particularly for goldeneyes, harlequins, scoters, and bufflehead—other species such as king eiders and long-tailed ducks are often difficult to decoy and are hunted from a drifting boat. First, the birds are located, usually with the aid of binoculars and often well offshore. An approach is made, and when the boat is upwind of the rafted birds, the engine is shut down. The boat is allowed to drift downwind toward the birds. As the boat approaches the rafted birds, they naturally turn into the wind to take off. Hunters stand in the boat and shoot birds that fly within 40 yards. This method is perfectly legal, provided the motor is shut down in time for all unnatural forward motion of the boat to dissipate before shooting.

Because most hunters fly to Kodiak from the Lower 48 and don't have the time to scout, let alone bring their boat and decoys, guides have become popular. Jeff Peterson (907-286-2252; www.kodiakcombos.com) is a seasoned veteran of Kodiak waterfowling who has been guiding full-time for thirteen years. Peterson is an Alutiiq Native who was born and raised in Old Harbor on the rugged southeast coast of the island. He offers both puddle and diving duck hunting throughout the season, specializing in collectors' trips for full-plumage sea ducks in December and January. The hunting is over decoys from shore blinds both on the mainland and Sitkalidak Island, a Native-owned island offshore of Old Harbor. He also uses an 18-foot Boston Whaler surrounded by decoys for some of his offshore gunning. Peterson is a licensed boat operator and transports hunters in his 24-foot boat. Clients stay at a lodge or a bed-and-breakfast in Old Harbor. Kodiak is reached by daily jet fights from Anchorage. Island Air (907-486-6196) operates local flights from Kodiak to Old Harbor.

Another sea duck guide, Blake LaRue, is based out of the Whistler Cove Lodge (907-235-4980; fourlarue@aol.com). Whistler Cove is located on Uyak Bay on Kodiak's southwest coast. The lodge offers immediate access to excellent areas that offer the full range of sea ducks. Blake hunts from both boat and shore blinds and uses a hard-charging Chesapeake to retrieve birds. Whistler Cove has been in operation for four seasons, but LaRue had been guiding and flying in Alaska since 1976. Accommodations are in cabins that house up to four hunters each, and meals are provided in the main lodge. A charter flight out of Kodiak is required, which runs about $100 per person each way. LaRue offers sea duck hunting between early December and late January.

For general information contact the Alaska Department of Fish and Game (907-486-1880; www.state.ak.us).

The Down East Coast of Maine

For many, gunning eiders is the pinnacle of sea duck hunting. Common eiders are the largest ducks in North America, with Atlantic Coast birds weighing up to five pounds. These tough birds winter along the eastern seaboard from the Canadian Maritime Provinces to Long Island, New York. The largest harvest of eiders occurs in Maine, Massachusetts, and Nova Scotia. Collectively, these three regions account for more than 80 percent of the eider harvest in the entire Atlantic Flyway. Among the eider shooting locations, however, nowhere is the shooting tradition stronger than the Down East Coast of Maine. Roughly encompassing the region from Eastport to Rockland, the bays are filled with barren rocky islands and mussel beds that provide a rich source of food and prime habitat.

While some breeding occurs along the coast of Maine, each fall migrants from as far away as Labrador and Newfoundland join the local birds. The coast of Maine is an important wintering area. January counts in recent years have estimated the winter population at between 35,000 and 45,000 eiders.

While there is some hunting from layout boats and boats rigged as camouflaged floating blinds, the vast majority of the eider gunning is from sea ledges and rocky islands offshore. Many of these islands

A large tender boat hauls two aluminum duck hunting boats out to the shooting areas of Maine's Penobscot Bay.

below the high-water mark, as well as all offshore rocks, are state owned and open to the general hunting public. The best hunting is usually in the morning on the falling tide and again as the tide floods, when eiders are moving to and from the mussel beds.

Because the hunting often peaks when the tide is halfway through its cycle, the rocks that you hunt are often referred to as half-tide ledges. At low tide, some of the prime areas are well above the water and at high tide they may be submerged. Therefore, knowledge of the tides is mandatory, and depending on the rate of fall, a good half-tide ledge may be accessible for only a few hours each day. Strings of decoys are placed near these areas, and hunters are stationed on the rocks and ledges to wait for the birds to decoy. Blinds are not required as long as hunters sit motionless with rocks as a backdrop. Boats are used to access these ledges, put out decoys, and retrieve downed birds. When the birds decide to start moving, the action can be fast and furious, with singles, small groups, and flocks of up to 50 eiders decoying with regularity.

The season for sea ducks in Maine is from early October to late January. In addition to eiders, early season Maine sea duck hunting offers the opportunity to add white-wing, surf, and black scoters to the bag, while midseason or later is best for eiders and long-tailed ducks in prime plumage.

Because sea duck hunting is a specialized sport—requiring expensive gear and often taking place under harsh and sometimes dangerous conditions—it is not recommended for the inexperienced do-it-yourself hunter. Joe Lucey of Coastal Maine Outfitters (207-722-3218; www.maineguides.com/members/coastal) offers sea duck hunts on Penobscot Bay and accommodations in a restored 1830s vintage farmhouse. The package includes meals, transportation from the Bangor Airport, and hunting services. The most unique aspect of his operation is the use of a 50-foot crew boat, or mother ship. The boat, which is fully enclosed and heated, is used to transport hunters from the dock to the shooting areas. The crew boat carries two 18-foot aluminum skiffs that take hunters from the mother ship to the rocks, and then tends hunters while in the field. After a long, cold day on a sea ledge, it's heaven to return to the comfort of the crew boat for the hour-long ride back to the dock.

Another Down East operation is Rising Sun Outfitters (207-461-5419; www.risingsunoutfitters.com), owned and operated by Ernie and Lori Spaulding. They have been guiding sea duck hunters for ten years. They house their clients in a country inn and offer sea duck hunting from ledges scattered throughout Pleasant Bay near Jonesboro. They offer packages that include lodging, meals, and hunting services.

If you go between early November and late January, dress warm in layers and make sure you bring waders to keep you dry. For additional information, contact the Maine Department of Inland Fisheries and Wildlife (207-287-8000; www.state.me.us/ifw).

Puget Sound, Washington

Unlike the Atlantic Coast, where sea duck hunting has been a tradition for more than a century, along the Pacific Coast its popularity is restricted to only a few locations. In addition to Kodiak Island, the Puget Sound area of Washington has become popular with diver and sea duck hunters. This region stretches from the Canadian border to Seattle and is a combination of wind-swept straits and protected waterways interspersed with evergreen-covered islands and rocky shores. While the entire area delivers good diver and sea duck hunting, the waterways between Bellingham and Everett, including Padilla and Samish bays, the Straights of Georgia, and Saratoga Pass deliver some of the most consistent shooting.

A Washington state resident who's obviously hooked on diver hunting.

One of the most diverse arrays of ducks in North America winter along the northwest Washington coast. Up to seventeen species spend the winter here, including long-tailed ducks, harlequins, three species of scoters, two species of scaup, two species of goldeneyes, and a variety of puddle ducks. The reason for this is the available food resources, which range from offshore mussel and clam beds to estuaries rich in aquatic plants and invertebrates. Coupled with secure resting areas offered by the vastness of the region, this area provides prime diver and sea duck wintering habitat. Northwest Washington is about as far south as some of the sea ducks winter in any appreciable numbers, yet it has the proper mix of habitat and mild winter weather to support good populations of diving ducks. This region offers some of the best scoter, greater scaup, and long-tailed duck hunting south of Alaska and the most consistent gun-

A pair of Barrow's goldeneyes taken on Puget Sound.

ning for harlequin and Barrow's goldeneye in the Lower 48. This region has become popular with collectors seeking some of the species normally associated with Alaska and the far north.

Depending on the species, location, and time of year, much of the diver and sea duck hunting is from camouflaged boats anchored in open water and surrounded by a generous spread of decoys. Many hunters use decoys that mimic the species they are targeting. This is particularly important when hunting harlequin ducks, a nearshore species that decoys well to its own kind. Scaup decoys are the most popular when hunting divers, while scoter and goldeneye decoys are the most frequently used when gunning sea ducks in general. Most shoreline areas are private and the majority are closed to hunting. Points are the preferred locations where shoreline hunting does occur. Available also are layout boat and scull boat hunting, both of which are effective.

The Washington duck season is usually from early October to late January, sometimes involving a short split. Diver hunting is productive from mid-October to the end of the season, while sea duck hunting perks up around Thanksgiving and generally peaks after Christmas. Access is good, and launch ramps are well distributed. Be aware, though, that some tidewater areas are designated waterfowl sanctuaries and other areas have been leased for oyster culture, making it illegal to drop an anchor unless you have permission. These are navigable waterways, and you can run or drift a boat across them, but the bottom is leased for private use. These areas are generally posted.

Much of the guesswork can be taken out of finding the right hunting location and scouting the vast area by hiring a guide. Ben Welton of La Conner Guide Service (360-466-4749; www.trophybirds.com) has been in business for more than twenty years and offers diver/sea duck hunting. He hunts from a 17-foot camouflaged boat and uses a variety of hand-carved decoys. Welton offers day hunts and caters to collectors who during a three-day hunt often take nine or ten species of the seventeen available.

Mike Wolsky of Wings and Waves Guide Service (253-335-7399; www.wingsandwaves.net) has been guiding for four years but has been hunting divers and sea ducks on a regular basis for at least ten years. He uses a 17-foot sea-class model of The Duck Boat (TDB) and a layout boat and hunts Puget Sound, principally north and west of Mt. Vernon. He caters to collectors and can target harlequins, long-tailed ducks, scoters, and goldeneyes. In some areas he provides combination hunts. He offers day hunts that include lunch.

For additional information contact the Washington Department of Fish and Wildlife (360-902-2200; www.wa.gov/wdfw).

Chesapeake Bay, Maryland

Since the market hunting days, Chesapeake Bay has been a mecca for both waterfowl and waterfowl hunters. Historically, it was the most important wintering area in North America for canvasbacks, and even though their continental populations have declined, Chesapeake Bay still provides a critical wintering ground for this species. The cans that winter there leave their prairie pothole breeding grounds and follow a migration corridor that takes them to the Upper Mississippi River, where they gather and feed for a month or more. As cold fronts push south and food resources dwindle, they move east from the Mississippi Flyway to the Atlantic Flyway and Chesapeake Bay. Depending on the year, there are good num-

Large fishing boats are sometimes used for hunting sea ducks on Chesapeake Bay, but diver hunters often use smaller, well-camouflaged craft such as The Duck Boat.

bers of canvasback on Chesapeake Bay by late November, where they stay until early spring. Hunting between Christmas and the end of the season in January provides the best opportunity to bag canvasbacks on the eastern seaboard.

In addition to canvasbacks, a host of other diving ducks (including scaup and redheads) and sea ducks (goldeneyes, bufflehead, all three species of scoters, and long-tailed ducks) either winter on the bay or pass through on their way south. The other divers arrive in earnest beginning in mid-October, with peak populations present about the time the cans arrive. Surprisingly, the first scoters arrive in late

September, and the best scoter gunning occurs from opening day in early October through mid-November. In early November, a good percentage of the scoters start heading to more southerly wintering areas. Long-tailed ducks don't show up in huntable numbers until early November. From the time they arrive, long-tailed ducks dominate the sea duck bag until the season closes.

This vast array of diving and sea ducks is supported by Chesapeake Bay's shallowness, abundant food resources in the form of clams and other invertebrates, and submerged aquatic vegetation. There is cause for concern over the health of this habitat, however, due to the proliferation of bayside developments, pollution, sedimentation, and the low oxygen levels in some portions of the bay. With recent controls on building and the discharge of pollutants, the bay is on the road to recovery and in far better condition than it was in the 1970s.

It is no secret that the diving duck populations, particularly canvasbacks and scaup, have declined in recent years. In the case of cans, the season has been closed or highly restricted, and while the scaup remain fair game, the bag limit has been reduced. As a result, more and more hunters have started hunting sea ducks on Chesapeake Bay, finding them to be both abundant and challenging.

Sea ducks are hunted from boats anchored in the bay, with large strings of decoys set nearby. Scoters decoy well, while long-tailed ducks generally fly by to investigate but don't generally commit to the decoys. Boats used for hunting sea ducks range from 14- to 18-footers, with or without camouflaged panels, to 25- to 35-foot fishing boats. The first time I hunted from a 35-foot white boat with a 12-foot beam, I was skeptical to say the least. And when I was instructed to sit on the engine hatch cover and not move, I really couldn't believe it. But it didn't take long before the long-tailed ducks flew by in range and the scoters tried to land in the decoys. Diving ducks are not as easily fooled as sea ducks. As a result, very few divers are killed from the large fishing boats. They are gunned more commonly from anchored boat blinds, permanent blinds built on pilings, floating blinds, and layout boats.

Hunting access to Chesapeake Bay is governed by several regulations. To hunt in the Sea Duck Zone, which is essentially the open waters of Chesapeake Bay, including portions of the major rivers that empty into it, you must anchor your boat or floating blind at least 800 yards offshore. In addition, you must be 500 yards from other anchored boat blinds or permanent structures like bridges or causeways. The Gunning Rig Zone has essentially the same rules, but it does not include the rivers that enter the bay. In both the Sea Duck and Gunning zones, you must have a Maryland resident in the boat with you when you hunt. The resident can be a guide or an acquaintance, but they must possess a Maryland hunting license.

Other than several wildlife management areas, the shoreline adjacent to Chesapeake Bay is privately owned. To hunt shoreline locations you must have permission from the landowner. To build or hunt from offshore stilt blinds, you must have permission to build the structure from the landowner that owns the adjacent shoreline. These blinds cannot be more than 300 yards offshore. Special regulations govern the building of blinds on the state wildlife management areas. To hunt the shoreline or offshore blinds, a Maryland resident does not have to hunt with you.

To help determine the best location and hunting method, it makes sense for the first-time hunter to hire a guide. Last season I hunted with two guides, each using an entirely different approach, yet both proved successful. Captain Jeff Coats of Pitboss Waterfowl (410-838-7264; www.pitbosswaterfowl.com) has been guiding full-time for eight seasons and is the maker of Cork Gunning Decoys. The hunting is from a Sea Class 17-foot TDB surrounded by at least 8 dozen decoys, as well as from offshore stake blinds. While he hunts the full complement of ducks on Chesapeake Bay, Coats specializes in sea duck hunting in October and November, diver hunting in December and January, and brant hunting throughout the season.

The second Chesapeake hunt was with long-time guide Captain Norm Haddaway of Chesapeake Expeditions (410-745-5682; www.bayducks.com). Haddaway was one of the first guides on Chesapeake Bay to offer sea duck hunts from large fishing boats. He uses a 35-foot boat and sets several long strings of long-tailed duck and scoter decoys. The scoters and long-tails don't seem to mind the big boat and often decoy to within 30 yards of the stern. Both guides operate from the Eastern Shore, where there are numerous motels and restaurants.

For more information contact the Maryland DNR (410-260-8100; www.dnr.state.md.us).

Pamlico Sound, North Carolina

Pamlico Sound along the North Carolina coast is a massive body of water stretching more than 75 miles from Cedar Island to Roanoke Island. The shallow waters of the sound are protected from the Atlantic Ocean by Cape Hatteras and a string of narrow barrier islands. While Pamlico Sound was historically an important wintering area for diving ducks, primarily scaup and lesser numbers of redheads and canvasbacks, population declines and changes in migratory patterns have reduced their numbers. There is still an array of ducks present, and sea ducks—all three species of scoter along with some long-tailed ducks—have become the primary targets. Limited shooting for scaup and bufflehead is still available.

Sea and diving ducks are attracted to Pamlico Sound not only for the relatively mild winter weather and protection it affords but also for its abundant food supplies. Scoters, long-tailed ducks, and scaup feed

Sea ducks such as these black and surf scoters are now the primary targets on North Carolina's Pamlico Sound.

largely on mussels, small clams, and a variety of other crustaceans. The mussel and clam beds are scattered throughout the sound, in water depths ranging from 6 to 25 feet. Scoters begin to arrive in mid-October, and by mid-November they are present in significant numbers. Long-tailed ducks arrive in early November, with peak populations present around Christmas. Black and surf scoters are present in about equal proportion and account for 80 percent of the sea ducks wintering on the sound. The remaining 20 percent are white-winged scoters and long-tailed ducks. The sea duck season opens in early October and closes in late January, with the most productive hunting after November 15. The diving duck season is shorter and in recent years has involved one or two splits.

Sea and diving duck hunting in Pamlico Sound is generally from floating blinds, anchored boat blinds, and in some areas permanent blinds built on pilings. Boat blinds are the most popular and range from boat hulls painted black, with plywood side panels, to boats with camouflage panels that are designed specifically for open-water hunting. These floating blinds are anchored in areas where the sea ducks and divers feed or in local flyways, and are surrounded by 60 to 150 decoys. A larger mother ship, usually a 30- to 40-foot fishing boat, is often used to transport the hunters and the blinds to the shooting location, as well as set up the decoys and retrieve birds. There are locations in the shallower portions of the sound where permanent blinds have been built on pilings. County regulations govern the construction of these offshore blinds; some areas require a permit, while in others a permit is not required. Hunting is legal in the open waters of the sound, with a few restrictions. During the regular duck season, floating blinds and boats can be anchored anywhere in the sound. Before or after the regular season, when only sea ducks can be hunted, anchored boats or blinds must be at least 800 yards from shore. Some areas on the barrier islands are within the boundaries of national wildlife refuges or national seashores and are closed to hunting. These areas are posted.

Recently, I hunted with veteran guide Tom Jennette of Jennette's Lodge and Guide Service (252-925-1461; jennette@beachlink.com). Tom has been guiding for more than twenty years and is best known for his sea duck and swan hunting. We hunted sea ducks from an 18-foot boat blind anchored in the middle of the sound and surrounded by decoys. Jennette uses a 38-foot boat to tow the blind to the hunting area and to transport hunters. Once the blind is in place and the decoys are set, he backs off with the big boat and waits. He offers hunting packages with or without accommodations.

For more information contact, the North Carolina Wildlife Resources Commission (919-662-4370; www.wildlife.state.nc.us).

Catahoula Lake, Louisiana

Without question, Catahoula Lake, northeast of Alexandria, Louisiana, offers some of the most consistent and diverse diver hunting in the southeastern United States. This 14-mile-long, 3-mile-wide body of water covers 30,000 acres at full pool, attracting huge concentrations of both puddle ducks and divers. It is considered one of the top spots in the nation for canvasbacks and ring-necked ducks. The lake is owned by the state of Louisiana and managed under a cooperative agreement between the state, the U.S. Fish and Wildlife Service, and the U.S. Army Corps of Engineers. Catahoula Lake is a navigable waterway open to hunting. In the middle, however, there is a 1,000-acre designated waterfowl no-hunting zone.

Divers are attracted to Catahoula Lake primarily by the tubers and rhizomes of chufa and *Sagittaria* (duck potato). The abundant food resources, in combination with the sanctuary where birds can raft unmolested, create conditions that attract and hold significant numbers of diving ducks. Much of the lake is less than 12 feet deep and a good percentage of the water is less than 3 feet deep. The water level of Catahoula Lake is dependent on releases from water-control projects on the Little and Old rivers. Each year the lake is drawn down to allow moist soil vegetation to germinate. It is then reflooded in the fall prior to the hunting season. Some areas are not yet flooded early in the season, resulting in reduced hunting areas and limited access.

The first divers to arrive are ring-necked ducks, generally in late October. In November they are joined by canvasbacks and scaup.

A flat-bottomed boat with a Go-Devil motor is the vessel of choice for negotiating Catahoula Lake's shallow waters.

Diver numbers generally peak in mid-December. Recent winter population surveys have counted up to 98,000 canvasbacks, 58,000 ring-necked ducks, and 10,000 lesser scaup. Add a handful of redheads, bufflehead, hooded mergansers, and ruddy ducks and you have the potential for a serous mixed bag of divers. The season generally starts in mid-November and closes in late January and often includes a split. The best diver hunting is usually from Thanksgiving to the end of the season in January.

The vast majority of the hunting on Catahoula Lake for both divers and puddle ducks is from floating blinds. Most are frames covered with grass or vegetation designed to completely conceal a boat. They are anchored in place early in the season and surrounded by plenty of decoys—from 100 to more than 1,000. The floating blind is left out all season, often in one place, although it might be towed to a new location if local flight patterns or use areas change. These floating blinds are built so a boat can be pulled into the center, secured, and used as a shooting platform. Birds shot and killed can be picked up by a dog or, in some areas, by wading. If a cripple needs to be chased, the boat can be pulled out of the blind and used to run it down. Additionally, some hunters put up stilt blinds built on 4x4 posts or pilings, and a few hunters use boat blinds with camouflage panels.

I hunted Catahoula Lake with veteran guide Greg Andrus of Catahoula Lake Guide Service (318-448-0732; www.duckhunt-louisiana.com), who has been guiding on the lake for nearly thirty years and has a solid reputation. He offers puddle and diving duck hunts from boat blinds as well as stationary blinds and uses an 18-foot flat-bottom boat with a Go-Devil motor to negotiate the shallow lake. Andrus takes a maximum of four hunters. Most hunters stay in Alexandria, where there are ample motels and restaurants.

For more information contact, the Louisiana Department of Wildlife and Fisheries (225-765-2800; www.wlf.state.la.us).

Laguna Madre, Texas and Mexico

The Texas-Mexico Gulf Coast is a major wintering area for waterfowl. More than 85 percent of the continental population of redheads winters here, along with good numbers of puddle ducks and geese. When it comes to shooting redheads, the Texas-Mexico Gulf Coast, and specifically the Laguna Madre, come out on top. The Laguna Madre is a vast, shallow saltwater bay protected from the Gulf of Mexico by Padre Island in Texas and a series of barrier islands in Mexico. Extending roughly from Corpus Christi to Boca Chica in Texas, and from below Matamoros to La Pesca in the Mexican state of Tamaulipas, it has two distinct segments. A good share of the hunting for redheads in Texas is concentrated between Port Mansfield and Port Isabel, while in Mexico redhead hunting is popular along its entire length. In Texas, the duck season is generally split, with the first segment in November and the second opening sometime in mid-

A good set of decoys near the right shoreline point can be a deadly combination when hunting the Laguna Madre.

December and extending into January. In Mexico, the season opens in early November and closes in early March.

Each year more than 350,000 redheads migrate from their breeding grounds. They make the flight in only a few weeks, stopping briefly and sporadically at staging areas along the way. By early October, before the season is open in Texas or Mexico, they arrive in huge flocks. As time progresses, more birds arrive, and peak populations are generally observed in late November. They stay throughout the winter, leaving for the breeding grounds again in March. The primary reason for this concentration of birds is the availability of food. More than 90 percent of the winter diet of redheads is shoal grass—a submerged aquatic plant that grows in abundance in the Laguna. It is also an attractive area for ducks because the Laguna is so vast that birds can raft in a number of areas with minimal boat activity and low hunting pressure.

The hunting methods used on the Laguna vary but have a tendency to be more temporary shore blinds and open-water stilt blinds than boat blinds or floating blinds. Because the Laguna is shallow and the tidal fluctuation is minimal, hunters conceal themselves with vegetation stuck into the mud on blinds that are built on 4x4s and pilings. Temporary and semipermanent shore blinds are popular and allow hunters the flexibility to move to redhead concentration areas. Redheads often feed close to shore or fly past points on their way to roosting or feeding areas. A good set of decoys and the right point can be a deadly combination. While large decoy spreads are sometimes used, about 60 decoys are customary. The spread is typically a combination of redhead and pintail decoys. The pintail blocks are used as confidence decoys for the redheads and to entice pintails, one of the more common puddle ducks in the area.

While there are plenty of do-it-yourself opportunities and most of the shoreline and the entire bay are open to hunting, hunters new to the area and those that don't want to fool with boats, motors, and decoys often hire the services of a guide. I've hunted with several, including Ryan Falls of Arroyo City Outfitters, booked by Fin and Feather Safaris (800-320-7117; www.finandfeathersafaris.com). Falls is a full-time fishing (redfish/seatrout) and duck hunting guide who spends more than 250 days a year on the Laguna Madre northeast of Harlingen. He boards his 20-foot shallow-draft boat and accesses the backwaters of the Laguna from a dock in front of his lodge or a launch ramp a mile away. The run to the blinds is fifteen to twenty minutes. He sets up several dozen redhead and pintail decoys off points or stilt blinds. Hunters stay in a lodge on the waterfront in Arroyo City that can accommodate up to six hunters in double rooms. Falls offers four-night/three-day hunting packages and clients can be picked up at Harlingen airport.

For more information, contact Texas Parks and Wildlife (512-389-4800; www.tpwd.state.tx.us).

Hunting the Mexican portion of Laguna Madre is a bit more complicated. Since 1989, a registered guide or outfitter must accompany all foreign hunters. This has effectively eliminated freelance or do-it-yourself trips south of the border. Booking hunts through an outfitter, however, does take care of the difficulty of securing the necessary hunting licenses and permits. Most Mexican outfitters are represented by booking agents in the United States, although some book directly.

I've hunted with several outfitters in Mexico and have found the hunting, food, and accommodations good and the transfer from the airport to the lodge painless. Pintail Lodge, owned and operated by Gage Outdoor Expeditions (800-888-1601; www.gageoutdoor.com), is located 80 miles south of the border crossing and 25 miles northeast of San Fernando, on the edge of the Laguna Madre. Lodge guides hunt both saltwater and freshwater areas. Flat-bottom boats are used to access the vast Laguna. Hunters are set up in shoreline or temporary offshore blinds surrounded by decoys. In addition to ducks, Pintail Lodge offers quail, dove, and goose hunting and can accommodate up to sixteen hunters. All-inclusive four-day/three-night packages include a pickup at the Harlingen Airport. The lodge maintains shotguns for clients to use, which takes the hassle out of importing firearms into Mexico.

Another operation on the shores of the Laguna in Mexico is Marina Del Rio, located near the village of La Pesca. The lodge and hunting program are owned and operated by Cavi Del Rio and booked by The Detail Company (800-292-2213; www.detailco.com). Del Rio hunts both freshwater and salt water, with redheads, pintails, and teal dominating the bag. Airboats and flat-bottom boats are used to access hunting areas where most action takes place from temporary shoreline blinds. Hunting for quail is available in the afternoon. Of the lodges in Tamaulipas, Marina Del Rio is the farthest from the border crossing— about four hours by van. The lodge accommodates twelve hunters and offers a four-night/three-day hunting package that includes a pickup at the McAllen Airport. The lodge has shotguns available for clients to use.

Other Diver And Sea Duck Hunting Destinations

In addition to the top ten destinations, there are certainly a number of other excellent locations for diver and sea duck hunting. While the list below is not meant to be all encompassing, it does provide limited information on additional areas where diver and sea duck gunning are popular.

From the look on this Lab's face, eider hunting is serious business between Boston and Cape Cod.

Other than Kodiak Island and the northwest coast of Washington, diver and sea duck hunting along the Pacific Coast is still in its infancy compared to the Atlantic Coast. A new operation in Alaska, booked by Multiple Use Managers (866-686-2527; www.mumalaska.com) offers sea duck hunting west of Dutch Harbor on Nikolski Island in the Aleutians. Collector hunts in December and January are sure to produce good bags of harlequins, long-tailed ducks, and eiders. The Seldovia and Kachemak Bay region near Homer also supports good wintering populations of diving and sea ducks. Seldovia Bay Charters (907-234-7498; buck@xyz.net) offers duck hunting from shore and floating blinds.

There is some diving and sea duck hunting in Willapa Bay on the south coast of Washington. Near the mouth of the Columbia River, which separates Oregon and Washington, hunting for divers, principally scaup and canvasbacks, has been popular for many years. Farther south, in Oregon, limited gunning is available in Tillammook, Netarts, and Coos Bay.

In California, the major diver and sea gunning venues are San Francisco and San Pablo bays, where offshore blinds have been in place for decades, and where good populations of canvasbacks, along with bluebills and scoters, winter. There is also limited diver and sea duck hunting along the north coast in Humboldt Bay, and diver hunting is available in southeastern California on the vast Salton Sea.

The western provinces and states on both sides of the Rocky Mountains offer some hunting for divers. Areas that support good diver populations, particularly scaup and canvasbacks, during migration include Beaverhill, Cooking, and many of the larger lakes near Edmonton, Alberta, where Black Dog Outfitters (780-662-3436; www.blackdogoutfitters.ca) offers guided hunts. Farther south, in Montana, portions of Red Rock Lakes National Wildlife Refuge and the state-operated Freezout Lake Waterfowl Management Area are open to public hunting. Red Rock Lakes is particularly good early in October when redheads and scaup pass through the area.

In Utah, the Bear River Marshes offer some diver hunting, as do many of the state wildlife management areas along the shores of Great Salt Lake. In Nevada, both the Ruby Lake National Wildlife Refuge and the Wayne E. Kirch Wildlife Management Area offer gunning for scaup, redheads, and canvasbacks.

The Midwest offers numerous opportunities for divers and sea ducks, including the legendary Delta Marsh in Manitoba and Lake Saint-Pierre, a 220-square-mile widening of the St. Lawrence River in Quebec where sea ducks and divers are gunned from sink boxes. Other areas include the Lower Saint Lawrence, the shorelines of Lake Michigan and Lake Huron, the Detroit River, and Lake St. Clair. Many of the larger lakes in Minnesota, including Thief Lake, plus other large lakes in Minnesota and Wisconsin, support decent diver populations during the fall migration. The Finger Lakes of New York are an important migration area for canvasbacks. Farther west, Devils Lake, North Dakota, hosts good diver populations where Northern Flight Guide Service (701-662-5996; www.take-em.com) offers diver hunting, with the best action early in the season.

On the mid-continent wintering grounds, good concentrations of divers can be found in the Atchafalaya Basin and Lakes Pontchartrain and Borgne in Louisiana. On the Upper Gulf Coast of Texas, Bay Prairie Outfitters and Lodge (800-242-1374; www.texas-goose-hunting.com) offers hunts for redheads on Matagorda Bay.

The opportunities are extensive along the eastern seaboard, where sea duck hunting was born. Starting in the north, the bays and near-shore waters of New Brunswick and Nova Scotia offer excellent gunning for divers and sea ducks. Goldeneye Guide Service (902-889-3187; seaduckmason@aol.com) near Halifax, Nova Scotia, offers shoreline and sink box shooting for scaup and sea ducks. In addition to the coast of Maine, Atlantic Coast gunning venues include the waters off the coast of Massachusetts, and more specifically the area from Boston to Cape Cod where East Coast Guide Service (508-336-3755; www.seaduckhunt.com) offers layout boat, shoreline, and boat blind shoots for a variety of species, including eiders, scoters, long-tailed ducks, and bluebills. Other time-tested areas where sea ducks reign supreme include the waters off Long Island, New York; Cape May, New Jersey; and Ocean City, Maryland. Farther south, the Eastern Shore of Virginia serves up divers and sea ducks, as does Currituck Sound in North Carolina. Even farther south, fair winter populations of divers can be found on Apalachee Bay and Lakes Okeechobee and Kissimmee in Florida.

Chapter Three

HUNTING TACTICS

When Ryan Falls and I left the boat dock, our intention was to do some scouting near one of the offshore stilt blinds that Ryan had used successfully a week earlier. About halfway to our intended destination Ryan pointed out a spit of land that barely reached into the laguna. At first glance it looked like the other points scattered around the periphery of the vast Laguna Madre. As we motored closer, however, a flock of twenty redheads flushed only yards from the point. As we came to shallow water, I jumped out of the boat and found myself standing in a bed of shoal grass only 10 yards from the point. That was great news, because most of the grass beds were several hundred yards from shore.

Guide Ryan Falls tosses out a decoy on Texas' Laguna Madre.

There were a few salt-tolerant plants on the exposed ground, which was nearly white with salt crystals. A passing flock of redheads was all Ryan and I needed to make plans to return the next morning. We returned before daylight, as planned, with 6 dozen decoys and fashioned a makeshift low-profile blind of driftwood and vegetation. Ryan quieted Buck, his Chesapeake Bay retriever, as we waited for dawn to arrive. As the sun began to paint the sky a light crimson, the first knot of redheads dropped into the decoys at warp speed. Half the birds put on the brakes to land, while the others came in so fast they had to bank hard left and come around a second time or risk crashing into the shallow water. A drake was only a few feet off the water when Ryan raised his shotgun and, with a single blast pulled the rug out from under the decoying bird. My shots were less focused; it took two rounds to anchor a drake that tried to escape our ambush. Buck was sent to retrieve, and soon the first redheads of the new day were in hand.

We finished the morning easily, bagging our limit of two redheads each plus a bonus scaup and a trio of wigeon. Afterwards we watched flock after flock of redheads buzz the decoys, land among the blocks, or fly around for a second look before continuing to some distant feeding ground. Some birds started diving within seconds after they landed, validating our hypothesis that the grass bed was indeed a feeding area. When we left, we dismantled the makeshift blind, picked up our empty shell casings, and left the redheads to feed on the shoal grass that grew near our newly named "Grass Point."

Every time I head for a familiar location or a new area—whether I'm outfitted with a boat blind filled with decoys or just waders and a few decoys—I'm always looking for ways to put my experiences to work. If you remain flexible and apply tactics that match the hunting scenario, you'll find that more ducks will come to your decoys. Don't get locked into one type of hunting. There are numerous tactics and methods to take divers and sea ducks, and using the full range will bring rewards. Keep a log of your hunts for future reference—recording weather conditions, hunting locations, flight patterns, date, species bagged, and other pertinent information. This data will reveal patterns of what worked and what didn't and will help you to become a more effective duck hunter. The tactics and methods we are about to explore have proved effective over time, in various locations, and under a variety of conditions.

Hunting Marshes and Swamps

Marshes and swamps are the most wide-spread habitats characterized as wetlands in North America. These areas vary in size from a few acres to several thousand. They are found from the tundra of Alaska and potholes of prairie Canada in the North to the Gulf Coast marshes of Louisiana in the South, and from the Atlantic Coast salt marshes in the East to the tule marshes of California's Central Valley. They are incredibly diverse and include both public and private wetlands that provide habitat for waterfowl throughout their annual cycle. These wetlands are

A freelance hunter can often carry all the gear he needs to hunt divers in a marsh.

the primary areas where many of us go to hunt puddle ducks. But they also harbor good numbers of divers (canvasbacks, redheads, bluebills, and ringnecks), as well as some sea ducks (buffleheads, goldeneyes, and mergansers).

Compared with big-water areas that generally require a boat and motor, lots of decoys, and a mountain of gear, marshes and swamps lend themselves to the freelance hunter. Alone or with a buddy, hunters head to the marshes on foot or in small boats, bringing with them small- to medium-sized decoy spreads and a limited amount of gear.

I have seen numerous areas where ringnecks, which tend to feed in shallower water than the other divers, were feeding alongside mallards, wigeon, and pintails. I've also seen marshes where mallards were preening and resting in deep water while only yards away redheads were diving and feeding. In these areas, the addition of a dozen diver decoys to your mallard spread will bring in divers, adding a new dimension to your bag.

Even on many public areas where puddle ducks are the most numerous species, if you seek out the habitat favored by diving ducks, the percentage of divers in the bag will increase significantly. Look for the larger open-water areas within a marsh and locations where shallow water drops off into deeper pools. Also be on the lookout for submerged aquatic vegetation, which is a prime diver food and grows in water too deep for emergent vegetation such as cattails and bulrushes. Divers also feed on invertebrates, so be on the lookout for ducks surfacing from a dive with a clam or other invertebrates in their mouth.

In prairie pothole country, some of the best canvasback, redhead, and scaup hunting areas are the deeper potholes. Surrounded by a margin of cattails, the center of the pond slopes away from the margin, creating a bowl-shaped pond. Divers will use deeper water to feed on the abundant pondweeds, and then move to the sheltered edges to rest and preen. Regardless of the area you select or the species you target, the secret is to figure out the high-use areas for the various species during the course of a typical day. Once that is determined, you can set up in a feeding or roost area or along a local flyway to intercept birds as they move between areas.

Nothing beats setting up where you have seen birds the day before. This can be accomplished by a freelance hunter who moves about the marsh in an opportunistic manner. A good example of this was my

To target divers in pothole country, set up in the deeper potholes or where the shallow water drops off into deeper pools.

selection of an out-of-the-way pond on a public area in Nevada that held a tremendous number and variety of diving ducks and delivered quality shooting. Marsh hunters who are flexible and carrying only enough gear to be able to move quickly have a decisive advantage over those who hunt on big water.

Many marshes and swamps are also well suited to fixed-blind hunting. In this scenario the ducks come to you rather than you moving to the ducks. With a fixed blind comes comfort, and it is less demanding than trying to figure out where to go or second-guess where other hunters may be. And most of the hard work is done before the season even starts. The selection of a fixed-blind location should be made only after studying the area and making sure ducks are using it on a regular basis. Many of the best locations will already have blinds or there may have been a blind in the general vicinity in the past. Look for old blind frames or the remains of a steel barrel sunk into a sandbar. That's not to say that local conditions, water levels, flight patterns, and food availability don't change on an annual or even seasonal basis, rendering many blind sites worthless. Do your homework and be sure you have a viable location before spending the time, effort, and expense of building a fixed structure. If you intend to build a fixed blind on a public area, make sure you know the regulations governing such activity and adhere to them.

The most glaring drawback of a fixed blind is the inherent inability to move it. What happens if the ducks don't come to your blind, which is bound to happen at times? Overall, the best approach to hunting diving ducks in marshes and swamps is to use a combination of freelancing and fixed-blind hunting, changing tactics as bird movements and conditions dictate.

Flat-bottom boats like this one with a Go-Devil motor are perfect for getting in and out of shallow swamps and marshes.

Whether your destination is a patch of cattails or an elaborate fixed blind, you will need some means of transportation to reach the area. Some marshes lend themselves to wading, and a boat would be more of a liability than an asset. In this case a good set of waders, preferably one of the brands with a printed camouflage pattern, will do just fine. Either boot-foot waders or stocking-foot waders with a good wading boot will work. Just make sure the boots fit properly—not so loose that they slip off and not so tight they cut off circulation and make your feet cold. When wading, it will be necessary to carry your gear or pull a small boat with you. If you carry your gear, use a mesh decoy bag with shoulder straps, and use a sling on your shotgun.

Other means of transportation include all terrain vehicles (ATVs). They can get you to the edge of a marsh and can go in shallow water for long distances. A variety of boats are useful when hunting marshes. These vary from small plastic or fiberglass models that are suited to hauling decoys and minimal gear to johnboats, canoes, pirogues, and other craft that are designed to carry people, dogs, and equipment. Keep in mind that some areas may be difficult to reach, so a smaller boat will make it much easier than a large one. Various forms of propulsion are used with small boats, including outboards with props or jet drives, electric motors, Go-Devil motors, paddles, and push poles. Your mode of transportation must fit the terrain and local conditions. Some of these boats can be fitted with a portable boat blind, which simplifies the concealment portion of the equation.

When hunting in marshes and swamps the use of camouflage clothing is important. The hunter in a boat blind anchored in the middle of an estuary might get by with staying low and wearing drab clothing, but a hunter standing next to a clump of dry cattails needs to blend in as much as possible. I mentioned using waders with a camouflage pattern, but the camo pattern is even more important when it comes to outerwear. Depending on the type of habitat, two good all-around choices of camouflage patterns are Advantage Wetlands and Mossy Oak Shadow Grass. If you hunt primarily in cattails or cornfields, a more specialized pattern might be appropriate. Make sure you have a parka or coat with large shell pockets, a hood, and a Gore-Tex or other breathable waterproof lining to keep you dry. A camouflage facemask or camo face paint can be an asset, especially where ducks are heavily hunted. Their use can prevent a shiny face from flaring the birds at the last minute. A portable and collapsible stool can make the hours in a marsh a bit more comfortable.

Hunting marshes and swamps in northern areas is productive until freeze-up, when open water is no longer part of the equation. Late in the season it pays to look for pockets of open water and areas that stay open due to currents or underwater springs, as they are often great spots for goldeneyes and other hardy divers that remain in the area all winter. On the wintering grounds, most marshes and swamps can provide continuous action throughout the season.

Hunting Lakes and Reservoirs

Big water is the domain of the diver and sea duck hunter. Although puddle duck hunters certainly kill their share of birds on lakes and reservoirs, when big water is mentioned most hunters think of hunting for divers. The classic image that comes to mind is one of a camouflaged boat surrounded by a spread of 200 decoys and a flock of hard-charging bluebills flying in close over the blocks. This is the stuff diver hunting is made of.

Puddle ducks use these deeper bodies of water primarily for security. They may sleep, preen, or even perform courtship activity on a large body of water, but they generally feed in marshes, flooded agricultural fields, or flooded timber. Sure, some dabbling ducks feed along the shallow edges of lakes and reservoirs, but they loaf on deep water much more consistently. In contrast, divers and some sea ducks use lakes and reservoirs for the full spectrum of their daily activities, including loafing and feeding. They may never leave the confines of the lake. And

Sometimes a bare shoreline and camouflage clothing are all the concealment a free-lancer needs to take divers on big-water lakes and reservoirs.

even when they jump from one lake to another, they are tied to these big-water areas for food and safety.

Hunters have capitalized on this behavior since the market hunting days by developing techniques that consistently put birds in the bag. Like marsh hunting, popular methods include both freelance expeditions (moving around the lake and setting up from a shore-based location or anchored boat) and fixed-blind hunting in areas of known diver duck concentrations. In the case of freelance hunting, it's important to be flexible and move quickly in order to maintain a high level of success.

On a recent hunt at Minnesota's Lake of the Woods, it took three moves during the same day to finally get into the action. We started out hunting a point on a small island near the Minnesota side of the lake. It looked like a perfect location: a wild rice bed in a sheltered cove behind a point. We set up 4 dozen bluebill decoys, and then found a spot along the rocky shoreline where our guide, Frank Walsh,

When hunting from lakeshores, freelance waterfowlers can fashion makeshift blinds out of local materials such as driftwood and rocks.

fashioned a makeshift blind of driftwood and rocks. By the time the sun had been up for about an hour, the only birds that came in were a pair of bufflehead. We decided not to waste any more time and picked up the rig and moved to another point—this time on the Ontario side of the lake. We gave it another hour, but the action was slow. We did, however, see several flocks of bluebills drop into a distant cove back on the Minnesota side. Again we picked up and moved. This time it was a point jutting into a narrow portion of the lake. Even before we had all the decoys set and the boat out of the way, a flock of scaup buzzed the spread. Once the boat was clear of the decoys, the birds came in fast and furious, and it wasn't long until we had our limits. The key to success was our mobility and not allowing ourselves to believe that things would get better if we stayed put. The first location was selected because Frank had smacked the bluebills there only a few days earlier. When it didn't happen again, we kept looking for a better spot.

Most freelancers who hunt big water use a boat. If you're setting up next to a bank or island where there is cover, pull the boat into or next to the cover. In many areas, the cover is sparse or it may be necessary to anchor the boat in open water to intercept birds as they travel along local flyways. In such cases, a good option is a boat blind with a frame that allows you to attach natural vegetation or camouflage materials. The boat is a necessary tool to transport hunters and gear, set out decoys, and retrieve birds, but it also can be used to find new spots on the lake or reservoir. If things don't go according to plan, it's often wise for one hunter to stay with the decoys while the other jumps in the boat and looks for birds rafted up or working other areas. Once the birds are located, you can move to them and set up. In open water, a boat blind, layout boat, or scull boat may be the only way to get at the birds.

With a boat, big-water freelance hunters can go where the ducks are, setting up in open water and moving more quickly to a new spot when the birds are scarce.

Finding birds and hunting them on a lake or reservoir is certainly easier with a boat, but it's not an absolute requirement. Hunters without a boat can accomplish successful big-water gunning. Some lakes and reservoirs have roads around their perimeter. Travel these roads, stopping at various vantage points to scan the lake for ducks. During these travels, I've flushed ducks from a backwater cove, stopped and tossed out decoys, used available cover as a blind, and waited for the birds to return. When looking for birds, keep an eye open for sheltered areas, particularly during periods of bad weather and high winds.

Diving ducks are tough customers and can ride the waves for hours, but when the wind really blows, they eventually get tired of fighting the elements and seek more sheltered areas to wait things out.

When hunting from sparse cover, the important thing is to be still until the ducks are within shooting range.

Inside points (areas sheltered from prevailing winds by a point of land) or emergent vegetation (like a rice bed or stand of cattails) are good spots when the wind howls. Sometimes diving ducks will be right up against the point in the lee, and a well-placed decoy spread will draw birds in close. This same location may be avoided during periods of mild weather or when the wind changes direction. Always take the wind into account when selecting a hunting location. Even more than puddle ducks, divers and sea ducks prefer to both land and take off into the wind. I've found that the points that extend the farthest into a lake or reservoir are often the most consistent in attracting ducks as they fly up and down the shoreline.

No matter where you end up along the shoreline, concealment of some form (portable blind, natural vegetation, rocks, or driftwood) will be required. Sometimes the amount of cover needed is less than you might think. I have successfully hunted goldeneyes and scaup on the Great Lakes with little more than a single dead log and good camouflage clothing. As long as you don't move, many divers and sea ducks will come to the decoys even though you are in a relatively open situation.

Fixed-blind hunting is popular on many lakes and reservoirs, particularly those with a long-standing tradition of use by ducks during migration or wintering periods. Many of these areas are in favored roosting or feeding locales where birds come year after year as long as the food holds out or heavy hunting pressure doesn't drive them away. If hunting pressure appears to be affecting their daily movements and you have control over how often a fixed-blind location is hunted, it's often best to rest the area by not hunting it for several days. This should help you avoid burning out the location where you've invested time and energy. Many duck clubs with fixed blinds restrict the number of days or locations where hunters can shoot so they don't drive birds out of the area.

Several types of fixed blinds are popular on lakes and reservoirs. Shoreline blinds are generally built from wood and covered with vegetation or camouflage material. Stilt blinds are camouflaged platforms built on poles or timbers over water. Floating blinds and boat blinds are moveable, but because they must be anchored and are generally surrounded by a substantial decoy spread, moving them requires effort. Some of the most elaborate and effective floating blinds I've hunted from are on Cataholua Lake in Louisiana. A 16-foot boat can be pulled into the blind and secured, making an excellent shooting platform. The blinds are surrounded by at least 300 decoys. These rigs attract birds that are feeding and loafing in the area. Under the right conditions, I've seen them draw in passing birds from impressive heights. Many of these larger decoy spreads are

Stilt blinds are permanent camouflaged platforms built offshore on poles or timber sunk into lake bottoms.

Floating blinds may stay in one location the entire season, but they have the advantage of maneuverability and can be turned to line up correctly with the prevailing winds.

left out for the entire season; others are brought in at the end of each hunting day.

Unlike fixed shoreline or stilt blinds, floating blinds ride up and down with the fluctuating water level and can generally be turned or rotated to line up correctly for the prevailing winds, even if the winds change during a hunt. Floating blinds can also be hauled in at the end of the season for storage and maintenance. While moveable, they generally stay in the same location during the entire season unless flight patterns change drastically.

Regardless of whether you freelance or hunt from a fixed structure, hunting the big water often gets better later in the season. As the season progresses, food dwindles in the smaller bodies of water, and where it's cold enough, they often freeze up. Larger lakes and reservoirs freeze up much later, if at all, and the volume of food often lasts longer.

Decoy visibility is especially important on big water. You can increase the attracting power of your spread by using oversized decoys and placing them where they can easily be seen. The spinning-wing decoys that have become popular in recent years can also increase the drawing power of your spread (always check regulations to make sure they are legal). The number of decoys used on big water can vary but it's often substantial. While not an absolute, early season hunters can get by with fewer decoys than late-season hunters. Like geese, divers

Greg Andrus, Alexandria, Louisiana
"Sometimes Fewer Decoys Work"

On Catahoula Lake it's common to use decoy spreads that number more than 500 decoys. These huge spreads are required to draw birds away from the big rafts of live birds and to compete with other large decoy spreads. But there are times when fewer decoys will work. According to guide Greg Andrus, "There are times when two large rafts of divers congregate on the lake. If you can set up a boat blind in between the rafts without running them off, fewer decoys (often less than 60) can be used successfully to attract the birds as they trade back and forth between the two groups. I add about 20 percent three-liter plastic bottles pained black with streaks of white. They roll easily and add movement to the decoys and won't turn over in wind or waves."

often respond to flagging, which is waving a dark-colored square or triangular piece of cloth on the end of a stick to attract the birds' attention. Once birds are committed to the decoys, set the flag down and get ready to shoot or the ducks will be by you before you know it.

Using boats on big water means there is always the risk of ending up in the water and getting wet and cold—or worse, suffering hypothermia or even drowning. Follow the basic safety rules of boating. Don't overload the boat, make sure the boat is powered properly for the load and distance you need to travel, wear life jackets, and carry plenty of fuel and a fire extinguisher. The major cause of most boating accidents involving duck hunters is weather. Don't risk going out when conditions are dangerous. The level of risk will depend on the size of boat you have, your familiarity with the area, and the severity of the weather. Watch the weather and do your best to anticipate major weather changes. If the wind changes direction and velocity rapidly, it may be time to start looking for shelter. Often there is a fine line between excellent hunting conditions and staying out too long, resulting in a long and treacherous boat ride back to the dock. With weather radios, the Internet, and cell phones, it's far easier to stay on top of weather conditions today than it was just ten years ago. By all means be careful.

Hunting Rivers

While rivers are widespread and used extensively by diving and sea ducks across North America, they are often the least hunted areas. Virtually all rivers are considered navigable waterways, and by definition, once you are on the water you can hunt almost anywhere you please, with occasional exceptions such as closed sections below dams and power plants for safety purposes or designated waterfowl sanctuaries. You must launch your boat at a public ramp or have permission to launch on private land in order to gain access to the river.

Conditions on rivers are more variable than on marshes or lakes and the birds have a tendency to move around more. Water levels fluctuate and you have to deal with currents and floating debris. From a safety standpoint, rivers can be dangerous, particularly during periods of high water. Some of the pools on the Upper Mississippi River that harbor large concentrations of divers are more predictable; they are more like reservoirs with a current. While river hunting can be a bit more complicated, hunting pressure is generally lighter than on many other areas accessible to the public.

Rivers are a freelancer's dream and can be accessed and hunted from either the shoreline or a boat. Shoreline access and hunting can pose problems because private land often meets the high-water mark, making access difficult. In this case, an ATV can be helpful. Once you gain access to the river corridor, ease along the edge of the river and, as long as the river is not running high, you can stay below the high-water mark. On some western rivers, I have accessed the river at a public launch ramp and then driven my ATV along the edge in shallow water to gravel bars or islands where I built a small blind or set up a portable blind.

To avoid trespassing on private property, many waterfowlers use ATVs to edge along the river's shoreline below the high-water mark.

The best way—and in some cases the only way—to hunt a river is by boat. Boats can be used to scout for birds, transport hunters and their gear, access hunting areas, and function as a shooting platform. When scouting, look for diving and sea ducks in backwater sloughs, along the shoreline where tributaries enter the main river, near emergent vegetation, behind islands, on gravel bars, and late in the season, below power plants and dams where the river stays open even during the coldest weather. All these areas hold ducks at one time or another, and a good decoy spread in the right location will provide action. The key is to stay flexible. Go to areas the birds are using and set up a blind as close to their major use area as possible. If the birds are rafting in the middle of a large river where access is difficult or hunting is not allowed, watch the flight pattern of the birds as they go to and from this rafting area and set up a floating blind along a flight path. In some areas like the Upper Mississippi in Wisconsin, boat blinds cannot be set in open water; they must be set in emergent vegetation. Be sure to check local regulations.

For safety's sake, a high-sided boat with a big motor is a must when hunting diving ducks on big rivers.

Boats used on rivers may or may not differ from those used on lakes, reservoirs, and coastal areas. I've hunted the Lower Columbia River for scaup from a boat that I've used for salmon fishing—a 16-foot V-bottom aluminum skiff with a 25-horsepower prop-driven outboard. Some rivers, however, necessitate the use of flat-bottom boats and jet drives designed specifically for running rivers because of shallow sections or heavy debris loads. I've also seen flat-bottom boats with Go-Devil motors (a motor that can be raised or lowered as the water depth changes) used effectively. Because there will be times that require you to run against the current and prevailing winds, a substantial outboard, plenty of gas, and a sturdy boat are good insurance. You may be making long runs to your hunting area and run into barge traffic and strong wakes, as well as floating logs and ice floes, making a high-sided flat-bottom or V-bottom boat a good choice. Life vests and running lights are required, and a spotlight can be invaluable. A dry bag with

Tony Toye, Boscoble, Wisconsin
"Bring Your Camo with You"

Tony Toye is a full-time guide who hunts the Upper Mississippi River. After years of trial and error he has come up with a quick and easy way to break up the outline of his boat. "A few years, back I started using what I call 'witches' brooms.' Witches' brooms consist of a willow stick 4–5 feet in length with a bundle of natural vegetation cable-tied to the top half. I carry 30–40 of these on the side of my boats on ladder holders. When we reach our location in shallow water, we deploy them around the boat, making for a quick and natural looking hide."

extra food, water, and clothes, along with other survival items, is a good idea. Bring a cell phone along for emergencies if there is coverage in the area.

Once you have reached your hunting location, take special care in anchoring your boat or attaching it to the bank. Use a good rope to secure it to a tree, and when anchoring, use lots of rope and leave plenty of "scope" in the line. Scope is the angle from the boat to the anchor and it should be at least 45 degrees, not straight down.

The boat needs to be camouflaged in some fashion. Some freelance hunters use blinds that are attached to the boat and can be folded down and out of the way. I've seen both Avery Quick-Set Waterfowl Blinds and the Pop Up Boat Blinds in action and they work great. Even if you have a boat blind with you, there are times that the boat will only be used to access an area, not as a shooting platform. Then it becomes necessary to get out of the boat and hunt from shore. Some of these locations may include a point or a gravel bar where you can use a driftwood blind or a rocky shoreline where the best hiding place is among the rocks. The beauty of being a freelance river hunter with a boat is the seemingly endless number of options you have.

In addition to freelancing, fixed-blind hunting is also a possibility on some rivers. Like fixed blinds in other wetland types, be sure the birds are using the area, and be positive it is legal to erect a permanent blind. The blind can be built on an island or along the shore and can be a simple or elaborate structure made from a combination of wood, vegetation, and camouflage material. Due to the frequent water level fluctuations inherent in river hunting, a floating blind might be the best bet. Unlike lake and reservoir hunters, who often leave their decoys out all season, most river fixed-blind hunters bring their decoys in daily to prevent them from being swept away by increased flows or debris.

River hunting success will vary during the course of a season, but there are times when hunting gets predictably better. Many rivers, as flow increases and water levels rise, overflow their banks and flood adjacent ground, including timber, farm fields, and other low-lying areas. While this is not as important for diving duck hunters as it is for puddle duck hunters, it pays to watch where the floodwater goes and see if birds begin using it. The freelance hunter can then make his move and take advantage of these high-water periods. Another good time to hunt divers on rivers is just after a cold snap that freezes many of the smaller marshes and even some of the larger lakes in the vicinity. Because of their flow characteristics, many rivers stay open when other areas freeze. Another good location is downstream from power plants and dams where the discharge water keeps a section of the river open all year. Many power plants discharge warm water, allowing sluggish rivers that would normally freeze to remain open even in the coldest weather.

Hunting Coastal Estuaries and Bays

Coastal estuaries and bays, along with other nearshore areas, are the undisputed domain of diving and sea ducks. While puddle ducks frequent salt water, especially black ducks on the East Coast and wigeon on the West Coast, it is divers and sea ducks that make up the vast majority of the tidewater duck harvest. The reason that divers and sea ducks are found in these coastal areas is much the same as it is for divers or puddle ducks in freshwater environments—food and safety. Divers seek out coastal areas, particularly on the wintering grounds where they stay for several months. Most of these areas are selected because of the food supply. Species such as canvasbacks that consume wild celery during the fall migration may switch to a diet of clams on the wintering grounds. These saltwater areas are prolific, producing great quantities of shellfish and other invertebrates that the birds consume throughout the winter. Eiders, scoters, and long-tailed ducks con-

Like humans, diving and sea ducks prefer coastal living. This hunter's set-up, across from Cape May, New Jersey, is a case in point.

sume essentially the same diet year-round, consisting of mussels, clams, barnacles, and other invertebrates that are abundant in salt water. Estuaries and bays provide large, open expanses of water where the birds can raft in safety. Divers and sea ducks are also hardy birds that can withstand the brutal weather these maritime environments sometimes dish out.

For decades, diving and sea duck hunting in the coastal areas has been a tradition, particularly along the eastern seaboard, from the Maritime Provinces of Canada to the Carolinas. The popularity of this type of hunting, particularly for sea ducks, increased significantly in the early 1980s when puddle and diving duck numbers plummeted. As a result, the Atlantic Flyway saw 30-day hunting seasons and limits of 3 ducks per day, including only one red-head and no canvasbacks. Many hard-core waterfowl hunters were not deterred, and they switched to the abundant sea ducks (scoters, eiders, and long-tailed ducks) that still main-

Bay hunters truly are a dedicated lot.

tained 100-day seasons and 7-bird limits. Even after the drought cycle and low waterfowl populations of the 1980s passed and puddle and diving ducks limits and seasons were liberalized, many of the converts to sea duck hunting stayed with the sport for its exciting, fast-paced action and the opportunity to see literally thousands of birds.

Compared to sea duck hunting along the coast of Maine in December, hunting divers in prairie marshes in October is child's play. It takes plenty of gear and know-how to hunt the coastal areas, including a boat and motor, knowledge of decoys and rigging, and an understanding of the tides. Safety must be considered at all times. Like duck hunters who frequent lakes and rivers, the coastal duck hunter has to deal with changing weather, bird movements, and the other dynamic factors that play a role in a successful day afield. But unlike his fresh-water comrades, the coastal duck hunter must deal with the tides—a dynamic force that occurs every day.

Knowledge of the tides is vitally important. At high tide there will be plenty of water to run your boat and reach shoreline hunting locations, but at low tide the water drops (at times significantly), and access within the bay or estuary is more limited. Many shoreline locations are left high and dry and are often great distances from the water's edge. High tides may also inundate some hunting spots, like the so-called "half-tide" ledges where eiders are gunned on a regular basis.

Diving ducks and sea ducks frequently move without any other stimulus in response to a falling or rising tide. Flock after flock of scoters or scaup, for example, may pick up and head in one direction on the incoming tide. It is likely the birds are moving to a choice feeding area where the water depths and currents are more favorable for foraging.

One of the first items a coastal duck hunter must obtain is a tide book. They are available at most sporting goods stores and bait shops in coastal regions or can be found on the Internet at www.co-

Ryan Falls, Arroyo City, Texas
"Don't Forget the Face"

According to Ryan Falls, who guides on the Laguna Madre, good camouflage works great but don't neglect face nets or paint. "I have hunted with hundreds of clients who were 'camoed out' to the max except for their face," says Falls. "And when I pass the blind in the boat, the first thing I notice are shiny faces. There's a reason you always see photos of Navy Seals with face paint—they don't want to be seen. It can get warm early in the season in south Texas and we find paint works better than nets or a mask."

ops.nos.noaa.gov. Once you have the tide book, learn how to read it. The best way to learn how to "play" the tides is by hunting with veteran hunters or a guide familiar with the area. Pay attention and ask questions.

Like the other methods of diver and sea duck hunting, you can freelance or use a fixed-blind location. The freelancer has a number of choices, including the use of shoreline hiding places. These locations range from natural rock formations exposed at certain tidal levels to a boat blind pulled into a stand of salt grass. Many of the best shoreline locations are on points of land that jut out into a bay or estuary. Where it's legal, I've seen hunters set up off the end of man-made rock jetties and enjoy good sea duck shooting. These points are productive because they reach into the areas the birds fre- quent and, when

This freelance sea duck hunter takes cover behind a natural rock formation and waits for the ducks to decoy.

used with properly placed decoys, can attract birds passing offshore.

The types of blinds used vary from tiny rocks, where camouflage clothing and lack of movement are all that's needed, to blinds made of local vegetation, rocks, driftwood, camouflage netting on poles, and commercially made portable blinds. Some hunters use a pond box—a plastic or fiberglass tub 8 feet long and partially covered with marsh grass—along points. You lie down in the tub, which keeps your back-side dry, and sit up to shoot. I've seen these used in areas where the

The Duck Boat, with its built-in pop-up sides, is especially made for open-water gunning.

tide is coming in, allowing successful hunting in water several inches deep. I've also seen layout boats, placed on a mud flat between two channels and covered with a camouflage net, used as an effective blind in an otherwise open area. As mentioned before, the key is to be flexible and use whatever concealment opportunities the situation presents.

One of the best blinds for the freelancer is the boat blind. Few and far between are locations where you can toss decoys out at high tide, shoot birds, have your dog retrieve them, and then pick up the decoys at low tide. Without a boat, your ability to move and change locations is limited. It can be used for transportation, scouting, to put out and bring in the decoys, and even if you have an excellent dog, there will be the crippled birds the pooch just won't be able to retrieve.

The boat also can be used as a blind and shooting platform. It can be pulled up to the shoreline, anchored in a salt grass bed, pulled into a tide gut, or merely anchored in open water and surrounded by decoys. Diving and sea ducks, particularly early in the season before they are gunned hard, will readily decoy to a boat anchored in open water and surrounded by decoys.

In Chesapeake Bay and other locations along the East Coast, 35-foot fishing boats with long lines of decoys anchored 30 yards off the stern don't deter birds from decoying. I have shot scoters and long-tailed ducks while sitting on the engine cover of these large boats. Most shots are at birds that are passing over the blocks, but in some cases the birds decoy to within 25 yards. Once a bird is down, the boat is released from the anchor (a float is attached to the anchor line to mark its location) and maneuvered toward the bird. As the bird comes alongside, a long-handled dip net is used to scoop it out of the water. The

A long-handled net can make retrieving ducks in open water a lot easier.

boat returns to the float and is reattached to the anchor, where the process starts all over again. No matter what type blind or boat is used,

> **Emile Vandommele, Port Rowan, Ontario**
> **"Minor Adjustments Pay Big Dividends"**
>
> **A**fter ten years guiding on Long Point, Emile Vandommele has become a student of diving duck behavior. "When I'm on the bay, I'm not only aware of how the birds are reacting to my decoys and layout rig, but I watch the birds that fly by and don't decoy. By making adjustments in the position of the decoys and boat or by making a short move, I can often put more birds in the bag. So, if what you are doing isn't working as well as you would like, analyze the situation and make an adjustment—even minor changes or adjustments can make a big difference."

it is important to retrieve all waterfowl quickly to avoid losing cripples and even dead birds that wind and wave action can cause to drift out of sight and become impossible to find. This is especially true for divers and sea ducks.

Boats specifically made for open-water hunting, like The Duck Boat (TDB), with a bit of marsh grass or camouflage material added to the gunnels and a generous spread of decoys, can be deadly. I've hunted from TDBs and similar craft and hammered scoters in North Carolina's Pamlico Sound and goldeneyes and harlequin ducks in Puget Sound, Washington. In other areas, tidewater boat blinds take various forms. I've seen nearly everything used as blinds in open water—from homemade barges topped with camouflaged wooden platforms to a ski boat hull painted black. In both of those latter cases, the boats were towed to the hunting area by a larger "mother ship" and then anchored and surrounded by decoys. The mother ship was used to tend the blind—placing and retrieving decoys and picking up any birds that were shot.

The truth is that almost any drab-colored floating craft with a good spread of decoys will draw sea ducks to the gun on the right day. Divers can be a bit more wary than sea ducks, but they, too, will decoy to open-water boat blinds with regularity. One of the methods used to draw birds into a spread of decoys in open water is flagging. The use of a black flag can be deadly on sea ducks. I've seen scoters, in particular, make drastic alterations in their flight path to check out the movement created by flagging.

The key to open-water boat hunting is to use plenty of decoys and to place your rig in a flight path or a feeding area. Generally, clear, calm days are the least productive, although I've had good action on bluebird days when the ducks were moving on the tides. Exceptions occur if the temperature drops significantly and triggers flight activity or if boat or barge traffic keeps the birds moving. (I'm not talking about the intentional movement or herding of birds, which is illegal, but rather bird movement as a byproduct of normal boating and shipping activity.) It is important to know the rules that govern the placement of floating blinds in a particular bay, estuary, or coastal location. These rules can vary significantly between states and even counties.

Another option for coastal waterfowling is to use a fixed blind. Like those used on freshwater, these blinds are found along the shoreline or, in the case of stilt blinds, in open water. The same blinds are maintained year after year. A fixed shoreline blind may be similar to those found on lakes and is built with a wooden frame and covered with vegetation, wood, canvas, or netting. In other locations, elaborate rock blinds have been constructed, generally on a mainland point or an island. One of the considerations when using land-based fixed blinds is the changing tide. Some fixed blinds are situated for either high- or low-water shooting. Others provide the best hunting midway through

Capt. Jeff Coats, Bel Air, Maryland
"Safety First"

Cold weather and open-water boating is no place for surprises. Jeff Coats, a guide and Coast Guard–licensed captain, says, "It pays to listen to the marine weather forecast for the portion of the bay or nearshore waters you will be navigating. Things can and do change fast out there, so be ready to pick up and go at a moment's notice. Every season there's at least one unsettling story of someone who was gunning somewhere they shouldn't have been due to lack of weather information, and ended up being a statistic."

the tidal cycle and still others on deep-water drop-offs that can be hunted at any tidal level. Know how the tide will affect the way birds use the site and plan for access to the blind as the tide drops or rises.

Floating blinds anchored in one spot are another possibility. Although used in coastal areas, this type of blind is not nearly as popular as it is on freshwater because the maritime environment can be windy, creating whitecaps and chop. When you combine wind with currents and tides, anchoring can be difficult. Therefore, most floating blinds in salt water are only left out for short periods—from several days to, on occasion, a few weeks—that coincide with a series of favorable tides or a static weather pattern. Nevertheless, there are some sheltered locations where floating blinds, ranging from small boats to large platforms, stay put all season. The obvious advantage of floating blinds over a stilt or shoreline fixed blind is that it can be moved.

Whether you like to move around or prefer to just travel from the launch ramp to the blind, you will need a seaworthy boat, and a motor that is big enough to push through waves and heavy chop. Depending on where most of your hunting takes place, it may be a 14-foot V-bottom skiff with a 25-horsepower outboard or a 40-foot diesel inboard. The choices are endless—just make sure the boat is adequately powered and is appropriate for the waters you will be hunting. Leave the flat-bottom johnboats, canoes, and small outboards at home.

Safety is always important, particularly when venturing out on large bays or estuaries. Be sure you have a dry bag with emergency equipment, including flares, matches, a flashlight, extra clothes, food, and drinking water. Personal flotation devices and running lights are required. Many boats are equipped with radios, but bring your cell phone if you are within its range.

Layout Boat and Sink Box Hunting

Layout boat hunting is among the most interesting methods of hunting ducks. First used during the heyday of market hunting, the layout boat quickly became popular with hunters targeting diving ducks. Because many of the areas frequented by divers and

Layout boats sit low in the water and are almost invisible to passing ducks.

sea ducks are far from land or are too deep for stilt blinds, the layout boat is considered by many hunters to be the ultimate floating blind. Unlike larger high-sided boat blinds, layout boats are built to be invisible to ducks until they are over the decoys and in shotgun range.

Layouts are wooden or fiberglass, wide-hulled boats about 12 feet in length, with an ultra-low profile. Due to their low center of gravity, they are very stable, allowing a hunter to enter and exit from another boat without the fear of the layout boat tipping over. Layout boats are customarily painted dark gray or black to blend with the open water. Most come equipped with a cowling, or spray curtain, that can be raised in choppy or windy weather to keep water out of the boat. As the name indicates, hunters lie on their back, with only their head elevated slightly to look over the deck for approaching birds. The boat is anchored fore and aft, with the bow (the more rounded end) pointing into

Hunters using layout boats lie flat on their back until the ducks are in range, then sit up to shoot at decoying birds.

the wind and the hunter facing downwind. The decoys are placed downwind of the boat, often with a string of decoys trailing behind to act as a guide for the birds that will be flying into the wind and toward the boat.

There's no question that layout boats are effective, especially in situations where birds are gunned hard from floating blinds, making them wary of anything that sits high on the water. In contrast to a boat with sides 2 feet high and topped by another foot of camouflage screen, a one-man layout boat sits only 8–9 inches above the surface of the water. This makes the boat difficult to detect until it's too late for the incoming ducks. I've had eiders fly directly over a layout boat, so low that had I been quick enough I could have hit them with my gun barrel. Ducks can get "blind shy" of layout boats, but it's rare, and if they do so, it's long after they stop decoying to conventional floating blinds. Layout boat setups are mobile, with moves accomplished relatively quickly by hunters accustomed to doing it.

It is important to keep wind velocity and water conditions in mind when picking the location for a layout boat shoot. While they are seaworthy craft, there are times when a layout boat is best left on the beach while you seek out larger floating blinds or a fixed blind. While the layout boat can withstand swells and wind, once the whitecaps start dumping water in the boat, it is time to pack up and go home. When layout gunning, be sure and have a life vest in the boat. Many layout hunters also have a two-way radio with an ear piece and keep in constant contact with the tender boat. The tender boat also can alert the layout gunner of approaching ducks he might not see because of his prone position.

Wind direction will govern what anchor weight to use, as well as the anchor placement and how much scope is used on the anchor. A dense rubber pad in the bottom of the boat makes lying down for several hours more comfortable. No matter how calm it is, you will likely end up lying on at least a wet pad, and quite possibly an inch or more of water. I recommend wearing either rubber boots, rain pants and a raincoat, or waders and a waterproof parka. I prefer to use my standard camouflage Gore-Tex parka and waders when layout gunning, but a drab-colored raincoat and rain pants will work just as well.

While layout boats were designed for use in deep open water, they are very effective in shallow water along the edge of a marsh or stand of salt grass. Often referred to as "grass boats," a standard layout boat is covered with marsh grass and anchored in shallow water adjacent to vegetation where it blends in and provides a shooting platform. Higher profile boats or other blinds would be less effective in these locations.

Despite all the advantages of layout boats, their use requires more gear and equipment than most methods of duck hunting. In addition to the boat, you'll need to own the associated anchors and ropes, a substantial decoy rig, and a tender boat to tow or carry the layout boat and transport hunters to the gunning area. Once the hunters are transferred from the larger boat to the layouts, the tender boat is then used to retrieve downed birds. I've seen even more-elaborate setups using a 30-foot boat to carry two layout boats and tow a 16-foot pickup boat. Once the layout boats are deployed and the pickup boat is untied, the mother ship moves off. The pickup boat waits well away from the layouts until shots are fired or the hunter signals to pick up dead or crippled birds. As you can see, the use of a layout rig can be complicated and expensive. There are guides in the major diving and sea duck areas that regularly hunt from layout boats. Booking a hunt or going with a seasoned freelance layout boat hunter is the best way to experience this brand of shooting before making a major investment. Then, you can decide if it's something that you want to pursue more seriously.

The sink box is the ultimate low-profile hunting blind— its flat top floats on the water's surface while the rest of it is hidden below.

While a layout boat floats on the surface of the water, and the hunter lies down in it, a sink box is suspended below the surface of the

Banned in the U.S., sink boxes are still legal in parts of Canada, where they prove highly effective for hunting divers and sea ducks on open water.

water and is attached to a low-profile structure that floats on the water's surface; it provides concealment below the surface of the water. In a layout boat you sit up to shoot; in a sink box you can sit upright or stand to shoot. The original sink boxes were made of wood and steel and were the blind of choice for the early market hunters specializing in diving ducks. There are tales of how effective and dangerous these unique watercraft were, including more than one story of heavy seas and rogue waves sending sink box hunters to watery graves. Modern sink boxes are made of a combination of marine-grade plywood, fiberglass, Styrofoam, and steel, and they are unsinkable, even if filled with water.

First outlawed in New York in 1838 for being too effective and unsporting, sink boxes became illegal throughout the United States in 1918 when the Migratory Bird Treaty Act was signed. Their use has remained legal in various regions of Canada. Today, most sink box hunting is found in Quebec, where they are frequently used on the St. Lawrence River, and Nova Scotia, where they are most often used in coastal waters. Still as effective as they were in earlier days, they are most often set in open water where diving and sea ducks raft. When a large decoy spread is added and weather conditions are right, they draw birds into point-blank range. And because the sink box lets the hunter shoot from a sitting or standing position rather than lying down, shots are more focused and precise. But make no mistake, sink box shooting can be a challenge in rough weather. Like layout boats, sink boxes rock and roll when whitecaps cover the surface of the water.

Compared to the use of other types of blinds, only layout boat shooting can even come close to being as complicated and time-consuming as putting together a sink box rig. Because of the expense and equipment required, and their limited legal use, virtually all hunters who want to experience this brand of waterfowling travel to Quebec or Nova Scotia to hunt with guides. If this type of gunning appeals to you, contact the Federation of Quebec Outfitters (800-567-9009; www.fpq.com) and the Professional Guides Association of Nova Scotia (902-889-3187).

Sink box hunting lends a historical perspective to duck hunting and is a unique brand of waterfowling kept alive in only a few areas. It puzzles me why sink boxes are not legal in the United States. They have about the same effectiveness as a layout boat and, as long as hunters obey bag limits and seasons, the kill of waterfowl would likely not increase even if their use were more widespread. Further, due to the expense and hassle of operating a sink box rig, not that many hunters would use them.

Scull Boat and Sneak Boat Hunting

Scull boats are long and narrow—generally 14–18 feet long—and manufactured in one- or two-man models. A very specialized watercraft, scull boats are propelled through the water by a single curved oar that extends from a hole in the transom. The hunter lies down in the boat and works the oar behind his head in a figure-eight motion to propel the boat forward. These boats are generally used without decoys, with the operator spotting rafted birds in the distance and sculling up on them. The hunter sits up to shoot when he is within range of the birds, and the birds are shot as they lift off the water. An experienced sculler can move his boat to rafted birds with precision and speed, often flushing sleeping ducks into flight when he sits up. I've heard some hunters say a sculling boat was designed to resemble a floating log, while other claims it isn't designed to imitate anything in particular; it is merely a way to remain undetected until the hunter is within range of the birds.

Some hunters look for rafted birds from the shoreline and then launch their scull boat and move to the birds. Others put their scull boats on larger craft or tow them behind until they spot ducks. After positioning the large boat well upwind of the rafted birds, the hunter gets in his scull boat and goes to work. It may sound easy, but it takes practice and determination to acquire the knack of rowing with one hand behind your head and still keep the boat moving in a straight line. Some hunters attach an electric motor or small gas outboard to their scull boat to enable them to return more quickly to shore or the large boat. It is illegal to shoot while the boat is under power. Therefore, the sculling oar is used to propel the boat on the "shooting run."

The best condition for sculling on a bay, lake, or estuary is a light chop—just enough to keep any noises muffled and to allow the boat to move through the water without a bow wave alerting the birds. If the chop and wind are too strong, it makes the approach much more difficult. If the birds swim off, and you decide to go after them against the wind, sculling becomes very strenuous and the level of success drops significantly. Therefore, most sculls are made downwind so that the approach occurs with the wind in the sculler's favor. Additionally, because ducks take off into the wind, they will fly toward the scull boat or to its side, offering head-on or passing shots. Successful sculling can occur in calm water, but the skill level of the sculler must be high.

Certain areas on the West Coast, the Great Lakes, and Atlantic Coast are popular with scullers. In these areas, it is particularly effective on divers and sea ducks, which are easier to approach in open water than most puddle ducks, and slower to take wing when surprised. The boats are generally made of fiberglass or wood. One-man sculls are more popular than two-man models.

Like layout boats, scull boats have a low profile and can be used in both fresh water and salt water as floating blinds when anchored and surrounded by decoys. They are very effective as floating blinds for sea ducks and, to a slightly lesser degree, divers. Their success as a floating blind, like most blinds, is greatly influenced by gunning pressure, weather conditions, bird concentrations, and location. They can also be covered with marsh grass and pulled into emergent vegetation or placed along the shoreline and surrounded by decoys. I've also seen them pulled up on a gravelbar or sandbar and covered with marsh grass. If a depression can be dug into the sandbar for the keel, they sit even lower and become a stable shooting platform.

Sneak boats were made famous on New Jersey's Barnegat Bay and were once a popular method of waterfowl hunting for divers and sea ducks. They are boats 12–14 feet long and are designed for two people—a shooter and a paddler. The paddler uses a short, wide single oar. Today they are probably the least-used duck hunting boat. However, a few sneak boats are used regularly on the Great Lakes and along the Atlantic Seaboard.

Unlike a scull boat, which is used to approach resting birds, or a layout boat, which is designed to be anchored in one location and surrounded by decoys, the sneak boat is somewhat of a hybrid. The sneak boat is usually towed to the hunting area by a tender boat. Once at the hunting location, a large spread of decoys (100 or more are recommended) is set in open water. The sneak boat is then anchored 200–300 yards upwind of the decoys. Hunters wait in the anchored sneak boat until a flock of ducks land in the decoys. The ducks are given a few minutes to settle down before the anchor (attached to a float) is released and the drift toward the birds begins. The oarsman keeps the boat moving in the right direction at a steady pace. A hinged canopy on the bow keeps the hunter and paddler out of sight until the shooting begins. When in range, the shooter drops the canopy and begins shooting at the flushing birds. Generally, only one hunter fires at a time, but with some practice, both can shoot at rising ducks if they are careful, particularly if the boat can be rotated sideways towards the birds just before shooting to allow each hunter a safe area to swing his shotgun. Earplugs are a must.

Old-timers who still use sneak boats have studied divers so well that they know how tolerant the birds are to an approaching boat and how much time a hunter has to get to the birds before they take off. According to Don Millar, who still uses a sneak boat at Long Point, Ontario, scaup are the most nervous and difficult to approach. Redheads are the most relaxed and allow the closest approach. Canvasbacks are somewhere between those extremes.

Sneak boat shooting is for the seasoned hunter who has plenty of time and patience, not only to set the rig up but also sit in the boat until the birds land so that hunters can make the sneak. To conduct a successful sneak boat shoot, it takes expert decoy rigging that provides holes in the spread for birds to land, approach routes for the boat, and quick, efficient paddling. The decoys must be set to hold the birds until the boat arrives, not just for the birds to fly by and take a look. If the wind is in your favor, it can be a significant aid to propulsion, catching the front canopy and pushing the boat toward the decoys and waiting birds. Depending on the strength of the wind, the trip back to the anchor buoy can be strenuous, with both shooter and paddler taking part in the chore. Sneak boat shooting for divers and sea ducks, under the right conditions and in the hands of a seasoned paddler, is a very effective method. Today, most sneak boat shooting is done to experience a bit of waterfowling history.

Pass-Shooting and Jump-Shooting

Pass-shooting is without question the simplest duck hunting tactic. Pass-shooting is little more than stationing yourself to intercept ducks that are moving from one point to another and shooting them as they fly within range. Decoys and calls are not used. In Europe, pass-shooting is known as "flighting" or shooting "flighted" ducks and is most often practiced in the very early morning and again in the evening after the sun goes down (it's legal there to shoot after sunset). Here in the North America, it has its place in both puddle and diver duck hunting, although there is generally more opportunity to pass-shoot puddle ducks.

The reason is simple: Puddle ducks fly over and sometimes feed on land. This takes their flight path over accessible areas. Divers and sea ducks seldom fly over land, although there are flight corridors that do pass over narrow spits of land or past a point. These are the areas diver and sea duck hunters should hunt if they are interested in pass-shooting. It's important to find a location where the birds are passing on a regular basis. Get to that location, use local materials for a makeshift blind, wear camouflage clothing, and use a face mask or paint to eliminate glare on your face when you look up. When the birds are in range, you bust out of your hiding place and shoot at the birds.

One of the biggest concerns in waterfowling, and it is especially worrisome with pass-shooting, is shooting at birds out of range. Referred to as "sky-busting" or "sky-scraping," it often happens because the shooter does not have the ability to determine the distance

A waterfowler moves through cover near a river or lake as he attempts to jump-shoot nearby diving ducks.

the bird is from the end of his gun barrel. Frustration can also contribute to this problem, eventually leading unsuccessful hunters to fire their shotguns in an attempt to drop a few of the high ones. Refrain from shooting at birds that are too high or too far away. Take note of the distance at which you or other hunters are consistently killing birds and don't shoot any higher. Sky-scraping cripples many birds that fly off, only to die later. In addition, it's irritating to other hunters who are trying to shoot at birds in range. Remember, the maximum effective range of even a 3½-inch magnum load in a 12-gauge shotgun (in the hands of most hunters) is still only about 40 yards. When picking a target, select one bird and don't flock shoot, even if there are plenty of birds overhead. The most successful pass-shooting is generally early in the morning and late in the day, when most ducks are moving. Still, it is wise to watch for major movement any time of the day, particularly during migration periods.

Jump-shooting is also a simple form of duck hunting. Instead of waiting for the birds to come to you, you go to them. The jump-shooting hunter wades through the marsh or along the edge of a lake or river. He either moves slowly and jumps birds as he comes upon them or observes birds ahead and plans a careful stalk. In either case, the hunter must walk or wade within range and shoot the birds as they take to the air. Jump-shooting is a more popular method for hunting puddle ducks than divers, and it seldom occurs for sea ducks. Because divers are often found in deep, open water, an approach on foot to within shooting range is nearly impossible. If you want to surprise divers, sneak boats and scull boats are the obvious choices. That's not to say the some species of divers that frequent shallow wetlands and streams cannot be jump-shot. I've seen ringneck ducks, ruddy ducks, hooded mergansers, and even a few scaup jump-shot with regularity in marshes in the West and Midwest. Some hunters also use a float tube or small boat to float down rivers and jump-shoot birds, although it's a method only used occasionally for divers and sea ducks.

The best time of the day for jump-shooting is midday, when the birds are resting. Be as quiet as possible, stay low, and use vegetation between you and the ducks as cover. Try to keep the wind to your back, so that when the birds take off they will be coming toward you for at least a few feet as they paddle across the surface to get airborne.

DECOYS, RIGGING, AND CALLING

N othing gets the heart of a dyed-in-the-wool diver hunter pumping faster than the sight of a tight flock of bluebills banking hard and coming to the decoys with wings cupped and feet down. The ducks come in because you are hidden and because they are gregarious birds, wanting to join a group of their own kind that has already found a good feeding or resting area. Decoys are the tools that ultimately bring the birds to the gun.

Decoys are an important component of nearly all diver and sea duck hunting; only hunters who pass-shoot, jump-shoot, or scull do not use decoys. Jump- and pass-shooting are better suited to dabbler hunting than diver hunting, making sculling the only traditional diver or sea duck shooting technique that does not use decoys.

Modern-day hunters began to use decoys almost as soon as they began hunting ducks in the New

Diver and sea duck hunters get serious when it comes to hefting decoys, as large spreads are more the rule than the exception.

World, and Native Americans used them more than two thousand years ago. But it wasn't until the market hunting days that decoys as we know them today came into widespread use. In the case of divers and sea ducks, the art of decoy carving and rigging reached its pinnacle in the late 1800s, when market hunters targeted canvasbacks and bluebills for the restaurants in the major cities along the East Coast.

Because diving ducks gather in large groups and often travel in larger flocks than puddle ducks, large decoy spreads quickly came into vogue as a means to lure these valuable birds within gun range. Many of the spreads were massive, numbering 400 or more decoys to resemble the huge rafts of divers that frequented the bays and estuaries. Today it is still common for serious diver and sea duck hunters to put out 150 decoys, which contrasts sharply to the dozen a mallard hunter might use in a pothole marsh. When you must deal with deep water, hundreds of decoys, and a rocking boat on rough water, the rigging portion of the equation goes from a 12-inch string and an old spark plug to multiple heavy weights, long and stout decoy lines, various

Mike Wolsky, Kent, Washington
"Use High-Visibility Decoys"

When hunting against steep banks, use plenty of high-visibility decoys. Mike Wolsky guides diver and sea duck hunters on the northwest coast of Washington and finds that dark decoys tend to blend into reflections of the surrounding background. This can make it difficult for approaching birds to see the spread. "I use plenty of magnum goldeneye decoys on the outside edge of my scoter decoys. The white on the drakes shows up against the high clay and heavily treed banks, adding a higher degree of visibility to the spread."

clips and swivels, and the problem of transporting all those decoys and their rigging.

Calling diving ducks is of minor importance compared to calling puddle ducks and geese. No one practices for the annual diver and sea duck calling championship since, to my knowledge, it doesn't exist. Diving and sea ducks, however, can be called, and under the right circumstances, calling can bring birds to the decoys that would otherwise pass out of range.

Decoys: Types, Sizes, and Species

Over the years, there has been a steady profusion of decoys made of various materials in assorted sizes and species. Most decoys today are hollow and made of thermoplastic molded resins, or to most of us, plastic. They are mass-produced by a number of decoy manufacturers and generally come in water-keel and weighted-keel models. Some companies only produce the more common species like mallards, pintails, black ducks, scaup, and canvasbacks. Others make a more complete line that includes more difficult-to-locate species like eiders, goldeneyes, and ring-necked ducks. Plastic decoys are lightweight, inexpensive, and painted with realistic colors and patterns. Most are sold by the dozen.

Diving duck decoys from Flambeau.

It is wise to choose weighted-keel models when selecting decoys for diver and sea duck hunting. Water-keel decoys allow water to enter the keel, which becomes the ballast to keep the decoy upright. They work great when set in sheltered water, but as soon as there are waves and whitecaps, water-keel decoys bounce around, tip over, roll, and do not look lifelike. When weighted-keel decoys are thrown out they have a tendency to land upright, whereas water-keel decoys often land upside down and need additional adjustment. The weighted-keel models will be a bit more expensive and weigh more, but most will be transported by boat, and the expenditure of a few extra dollars will prove worthwhile in the long run.

The main problem with hollow plastic decoys is their inability to float once they have been hit with shot. No matter how hard you try, there will come a time when a bird flies low over the decoys and you cut loose with a round. You may kill the duck, but you may also kill the decoy. It may not be evident at first, but eventually even one pellet hole will cause the decoy to sink at least partially and lose its effectiveness. The holes can be patched with various glues and resins, but too many holes or a shot at close range ruins them forever.

Herter's solid foam decoys.

Decoys like Herter's Model 63, sold by Cabela's, are solid foam and can be ordered with a hard styrene coating that renders them not only unsinkable but dent and scratch resistant. They have weighted keels and ride well even in rough water. The solid bodies are resistant to breakage, and if shot they continue to float. They weigh more than plastic decoys, which is generally not a problem for diver hunters, but they also cost more. Cork decoys are not as popular as they once were. Nevertheless, they are excellent decoys that are durable and can take shot. They ride lower in the water than hard foam or weighted-keel plastic decoys, are expensive and heavy, and are becoming difficult to find. There are still some wood decoys being used on a daily basis. They are usually made by individual decoy makers who cater to the small group of hunters who still use them. Wood decoys are much more expensive than even the best cork or foam decoys and they are heavy. But they hold up well, can take shot, and can be repainted easily. Foam and cork decoys are sold by the half dozen or dozen, while wooden decoys are usually priced individually. Floating silhouette decoys, often called V-boards, are used in some areas, particularly for sea ducks. Many are homemade and generally come in single and triple silhouette configurations.

When purchasing decoys you must consider not only what type to buy but also what size. Factory-made decoys come in three sizes—standard (15 to 16 inches from bill to tail) or about the size of a live duck, magnums (18 to 20 inches long), and super-magnums (19 to 22 inches long). The reason for the larger size is what I call the "visibility index." The larger the decoy, the farther away it can be seen by ducks and, consequently, the more drawing power it will have. The first use of magnum decoys in a particular area may produce dramatic results. After magnums have been used for a while and all the other hunters are using them, they often become a necessity just to compete with the other spreads. Nevertheless, larger decoys seem to attract ducks from greater distances.

The larger sizes are heavier and cost more. One way to cut the cost of putting together a large spread is to use two decoy sizes—standard or magnums as the primary decoys, with a couple of dozen of the next larger size to increase the visibility index. On the other hand, standard sizes are definitely the most practical if you have to carry them any dis-

---

Blake LaRue, Uyak Bay, Alaska
"Use Dark Decoys"

"**I** think dark decoys give the illusion of more birds on the water," says Blake LaRue, a waterfowl guide and bush pilot on Kodiak Island. "With thousands of hours of Alaska flying, I have observed many ducks on the water. When you fly over a set of dark birds or decoys, it looks like there are more birds on the water than there really are. I add decoys with white to my spreads to represent goldeneyes, oldsquaws, and eiders if I'm hunting those species."

---

tance. If you are hunting divers on a North Dakota pothole in October, 1 or 2 dozen standard decoys may be sufficient.

When hunting divers it is always best to imitate the species you are hunting. In areas like the Texas Gulf Coast, where redheads comprise 98 percent of the diver bag, many hunters use only redhead decoys. On the Upper Mississippi River, where canvasbacks are the predominant divers, stay with canvasback blocks, and on Lake of the Woods stick with scaup decoys. But many hunters who target a variety of divers, and can afford only one set of decoys, use a spread of scaup decoys because these attract most species of diving ducks. If you are hunting scaup but there are a few cans or redheads in the area, you can increase the attractiveness of the spread to those species by adding a dozen or two canvasback or redhead decoys without compromising the primary objective. The presence of a few canvasback decoys also adds realism and adds more white, which adds to the visibility index. In some areas, floating plastic jugs painted back and white can be used as an inexpensive way to increase the number of decoys in a spread. I don't care for the way they ride and don't use them myself, but I've met some hunters who swear by them as fill-in decoys.

When selecting decoys for sea ducks, it's also a good idea to buy decoys that mimic the species you will be hunting the most. Eiders usually feed and raft together and scoters generally are in the company of other scoters. Where sea ducks do mix, you can often attract multiple species by setting up a group of eider decoys on one side of the spread and scoters on the other. Long-tailed ducks (oldsquaws) seldom decoy, but a handful of oldsquaw decoys on the edge of a spread adds to the visibility index and, because of the oldsquaw's wariness, adds a level of confidence for other species. Some specialized situations (for example, hunting harlequin ducks in Alaska) may require a small spread of only harlequin decoys set near rocky shorelines where very few other ducks are found.

In many areas, both puddle ducks and divers are present and can be attracted to the same decoy spread. In these cases, it may be wise to add a few mallard or pintail decoys. Wigeon are commonly seen feed-

Empty plastic jugs painted black-and-white can be an inexpensive way to increase the number of decoys in a spread.

An assortment of eider decoys.

ing with diving ducks in some areas, and a few wigeon decoys will draw in the dabbling ducks and act as confidence decoys for the divers. When placing puddle duck decoys with diving duck decoys, keep the two species segregated within the overall spread. If possible, place the puddle duck decoys on the lee or shallow-water side of the spread. Geese sometimes share an area with divers, and the addition of a few goose decoys can help bring in the divers and a bonus goose or two.

There also are numerous special-effect decoys, including sleeper, flying, confidence, and motorized models. These are generally sold one at a time, although occasionally they can be bought in half-dozen lots. Sleeper decoys are floating decoys with the head folded back in the sleeping position. If you study a large raft of diving or sea ducks, you will often see several birds in the sleeping position. If your goal is to imitate a flock of rafted ducks, the addition of some sleeper decoys adds realism to the spread. Flying decoys are plastic decoys made with their wings outstretched. They are placed on poles that elevate the flying decoys over the water to simulate ducks that are about to land.

Confidence decoys imitate other species of birds in or near a spread. They can add realism and give ducks the extra incentive they need to come in for a closer look. Heron and egret decoys are used primarily in shallow-water puddle duck spreads. Swan, goose, gull, and coot decoys are placed among or near diver spreads. Some hunters claim that once a spread gets larger than 50 or 60 decoys, confidence decoys are lost in the overall size of the spread. But 4 or 5 swan decoys stick out like the proverbial sore thumb, and where swans are common, I truly believe they help provide realism and increase the visibility index.

Adding motion or movement to decoys has been one of the tricks of the trade since the market hunting days. Movement is more important on calm days, because wind naturally adds movement to the decoys. Puddle duck hunters often rig a decoy so that the head can be pulled under water to simulate a duck tipping up. Others attach a cord to several decoys and pull or jerk on it to move the decoys through the water. Because divers are hunted on big water, where there is usually some wind, diver decoy movement has not been developed to the degree it has in puddle duck hunting. Still, I've seen jerk cords used effectively for diver hunting. A bungee cord or piece of inner tube is spliced into the line (which is attached to a heavy weight) to give it elasticity. When the cord is jerked, the decoys are pulled through the water and then drawn back to their original position by the contraction of the cord or tube, giving the impression that the decoys are swimming. Jerk cords are best used to catch the eye of birds that are approaching or passing by, not birds that are in close or about to land.

More recently the use of spinning-wing, swimming, and shaking decoys has become popular. They are battery-powered and designed to add motion to the spread to increase both realism and visibility. Think

A spinning-wing decoy can help add movement and realism to your spread.

about how you spot most wildlife when you are in the field, be it a deer or a duck. If a deer is on the edge of the woods but stationary, or a duck is tucked-up against marsh vegetation but not moving, they are nearly invisible. As soon as the deer runs or the duck flies, they are easy to see. Motion decoys work the same way. Swimming decoys move around, and shaking decoys stay in one place as they vibrate or shake to disturb the surface of the water.

Spinning-wing decoys, often referred to as roto or moto ducks, have created quite a stir in the past few years. They are made to resemble a duck with its wings moving as if flapping while on the water or getting ready to land. They are powered by C-cell batteries, motorcycle-type batteries, or a 12-volt car battery connected to the decoys via an underwater wire. The batteries rotate the wings at a fast pace. Generally one side of the spinning wing is black and the other white. While spinning-wing decoys have been around in some form for many years, it's only been in the last few years that they have become popular. Today they are available in most species, including divers. Some hunters attach remote switches to turn the spinning-wing off as the birds come in close, and to turn them back on if the birds circle away. Other hunters run spinning-wing decoys continuously with good results. Clear and cold days, when ducks can see long distances, seem to be better conditions for these decoys than days that are rainy or heavily overcast.

Several recent studies have concluded that spinning-wing decoys are up to seven times more effective in drawing birds to the gun than decoy spreads without them. The studies were conducted primarily on puddle ducks, although in several studies any duck that decoyed became part of the database. In all cases, the effectiveness was the greatest early in the season. Like magnum decoys and various other new products, the birds can become accustomed to their use, and their effectiveness often declines as the season progresses. The use of these decoys has generated plenty of debate, and several states have barred their use or restricted it to certain times during the season. Before using one, check the regulations governing their use in the state you are hunting. I have seen spinning-wing decoys used when hunting cans and scaup, and I believe they attract birds. Some hunters feel their use is unethical, while others wouldn't go duck hunting without them. The decision to use them is based on local regulations and personal choice.

Once you have determined the type, size, and the species of decoy to buy, you have to decide how many to obtain. The size of the body of water, the distance it is from the vehicle, and how many birds have been using it will all dictate how many decoys you'll need. If it's a mile to the pond and there are typically fifteen or twenty birds on the water, a dozen is a realistic number to carry that far and still attract ducks. But bring all the decoys you possibly can when hunting from a layout or sneak boat, or when set up in a fixed blind. Here you are trying to pull in divers and sea ducks that will be passing offshore while in competition with rafts of live birds and other decoy spreads. Two hundred would not be too many, and I've hunted over spreads that numbered more than 500. Granted, the decoys were set out and left for the season, but at one point all 500 had to be set out. I've also seen 200 put out and taken in on the same day. Generally, the larger the spread, the higher the visibility index and the more drawing power it will have. Ducks like company, and if plenty of decoys are used, other ducks will fly in to at least investigate. But large decoy spreads don't always work. No matter how large the spread, when it's a bluebird day with no wind and huge rafts of live birds nearby, you might as well drink coffee and tell lies. Don't count on killing a limit of ducks. On the other hand, under the right conditions—overcast skies, wind, choppy water, lots of flight activity—a large decoy spread can magically pull in virtually every duck that comes by. More customary is something in between— the singles, pairs, and small groups will decoy and the larger flocks may swing by for a look but not actually try to land.

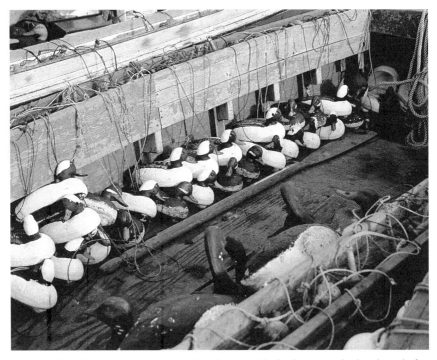

A mess of bufflehead and assorted other decoys with the lines attached and ready for action.

Decoy Rigging

Braided nylon line.

In most puddle duck hunting scenarios, decoy rigging is a relatively simple affair. When hunting divers and sea ducks it can be simple or more complicated. The term rigging applies to the attachment of a decoy to a line, which is attached, in turn, to an anchor that holds the decoy in place. The length of the line is determined by the depth of the water. The size of the anchor is determined by the weight of the decoy and conditions it will be used in. The heavier the decoy and the rougher the water or stronger the current, the larger the decoy anchor. Additionally, in rough weather the length of the line should be increased so that the line from the decoy to the anchor is at a 45-degree angle (or greater) to the bottom. Make fixed-length anchor lines at least two feet longer than the average depth of the water. Remember, it's better to have decoy lines too long than too short.

Several types and sizes of lines are used in decoy rigging. The most popular is nylon line, either twisted or braided. It's strong, rot-proof, sinks when wet, and is relatively inexpensive. It's available in brown or olive-green, both of which are better choices than white. Twisted nylon line has three strands, but it is not as strong or as resistant to abrasion and has a tendency to unravel. Twisted nylon comes in a tar-coated variety, adding to its abrasion resistance, rigidity, and enhanced knot-holding ability. Braided nylon is stronger than twisted nylon and consists of eight to twelve strands. When rigging decoys with nylon, melt the cut ends with a match or lighter to seal them off.

Line size depends on the type of rigging. If you are rigging individual decoys, chose nylon between #18 (.058-inch diameter) and #36 (.085-inch diameter). If you are rigging long strings of decoys attached to heavy weights, it's wise to use up to #60 (.116-inch diameter). The large sizes are easier to handle in cold, wet conditions while wearing a pair of gloves.

Other line material includes plastic extruded line—a green pliable plastic line sold under the brand names Avery Knot-Proof and Tanglefree. It is tangle free but can be difficult to handle in cold weather and does not hold knots well. Crimps or locking devices are used to assure the line stays attached to the decoy and the anchor. This line is most often used with single-line decoy rigs. Both coated and uncoated cotton lines are still used. They work well but are prone to rotting and deterioration over time. Heavy monofilament line also is used, but it can tangle and be difficult to handle in cold, icy conditions.

Anchors have one task—to hold a decoy or a line of decoys in place. Many kids have raided their dad's junk drawer and scrounged up old spark plugs for weights, and hunters have at times used bolts,

---

Capt. Jeff Coats, Bel Air, Maryland
"Use Heavy Decoy Weights"

"While open-water duck hunting, I have found as far as decoy weights go, the heavier the better," says Capt. Jeff Coats, a veteran of Chesapeake Bay diver and sea duck hunting. "There's no worse feeling than anchoring the boat and settling in to shoot only to watch your decoy rig slowly 'walk' away, whether it be single-rigged decoys or an entire main line. Old window sash weights are a simple and effective source of decoy anchors."

---

railroad spikes, or chunks of brick. Most anchors today are made of lead. The shape of anchor you use and how heavy it is will be dictated not only by water depth and conditions, but also by your method of transportation. If most of your hunting is by boat, anchor weight and type may be a minor consideration. If you have to pack 2 dozen decoys a mile, weight and transportability become a concern.

Strap anchor.

When rigging single-line decoys, lead strap anchors are popular. A strap anchor is a long, thin, lead bar that holds the decoy in place. After they have been brought in, the line is wrapped around the body or neck of the decoy and the anchor is wrapped around the neck. This keeps the line in place during transport and prevents tangling. Anchor size depends on the water conditions and type of bottom. A shallow marsh with a muddy bottom may require the use of a 4-ounce weight, while a decoy set in open water with a sandy bottom may require an 8-ounce weight.

Many hunters who rig decoys individually prefer pyramid or mushroom anchors for their ability to dig in and hold on smooth bottoms and withstand windy surface conditions. More care must be taken when storing these anchors because they have a greater tendency to tangle than strap anchors. Other anchor types for

Mushrooom and pyramid anchors.

single-line decoy rigs include neck ring, wrap-around, and grapple anchors. They all work and have their place. Their use is often a matter of personal preference.

The addition of large brass or stainless steel fishing type snap-swivels to single-line decoy rigs is popular when rigging diver and sea duck decoys. The addition of a swivel allows the decoy to move freely,

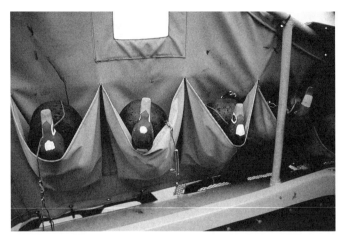

Scoter decoys with long-line clips attached.

Waterfowlers attaching individual decoys to a single main line.

eliminating line twist, and it provides a quick method to connect and disconnect the line. It also allows the line to be lengthened by snapping in an additional length of line with snap-swivels on both ends. Some hunters prefer to transport and store decoys without lines and anchors attached, and a snap swivel makes this easy.

Many hunters use several decoys that are attached to a main line when hunting divers and sea ducks. Generally 6 to 18 decoys are attached to a single line with a good-sized anchor at each end. If conditions change, multiple decoys on a single line can be moved all at once. It is often necessary, for example, to move decoys as the tidal level or wind direction changes. To accomplish this, an end decoy is picked up by hand or with a boat hook, and the entire string is brought aboard. If the move is close, the decoys can be towed behind the boat to the new location and reset.

Single-line, multiple-decoy rigs require heavy anchors. The type and weight are dependent on currents, wave action, and the weight of the decoys. Grapple and mushroom anchors that are 2 pounds and larger are often used for this purpose. I use 5-pound window sash weights for multiple decoy rigs. Sash weights are

Five-pound window sash weights make perfect anchors for single-line, multiple-decoy rigs.

available at some window or glass shops for free or at a reasonable price.

The length of the main line is variable and dependent on the number of decoys and water depth. Allow 6–8 feet between decoys, and make sure the distance from the first and last decoy to the anchor is at

Tom Jennette, Englehard, North Carolina
"Big-Water Decoy Set"

Aaccording to Tom Jennette, who hunts the open water of Pamlico Sound, "When selecting your main line for a single-line, multiple-decoy rig, use line that has body and not much flexibility. I use ³⁄₁₆-inch poly for my main line. This line is heavy, won't tangle, and is easy to handle. The distance between the decoys on the line should be far enough apart that in choppy waters the decoys won't hit each other—a minimum of 3 feet and occasionally as much as 10 feet apart."

least twice the water depth. Some hunters use large harness snaps like those found on dog leashes to attach anchors to the main line. The snap allows anchors to be quickly snapped on and off, and the weight of the anchor can be changed as needed. With this method, anchors can also be stored and transported separate from the decoys and main line.

There are several ways to attach decoys to single-line, multiple-decoy rigs. The simplest and fastest method is to attach a short length of line (6 inches or less) to a decoy and the other end to a long-line clip. The long-line clip is squeezed open and attached to the main line. Long-

A canvasback decoy attached to a long-line clip.

A spread of single-line, multiple-decoy rigs.

Don Millar, Port Rowan, Ontario
"Use Long-Line Clips"

Don Millar, who has guided on Long Point for more than thirty years, has come up a system that makes putting out and bringing in decoys easy, even if it's cold and you are wearing gloves. "I use a ⅜-inch nylon main line attached to 5-pound sash weights on each end. I drop the first weight in the water and then attach decoys to the main line at 4- to 5-foot intervals. Each decoy is rigged with 300-pound monofilament line 18 inches in length. The line is secured to the decoy on one end and to a long-line clip on the other. After I have clipped 15 decoys to the main line, I toss the second weight over the side. When the rig needs to be picked up, just snap off the long-line clips."

Mike Wolsky, Kent, Washington
"Stagger Decoys"

Guide Mike Wolsky suggests staggering decoys when putting them out on main lines. "Put four or five close together, leave 15 feet of space, and then put two or three more," says Wolsky. He finds that where he hunts in Puget Sound, changing the spacing of decoys creates a more realistic look to the spread. Try to stay away from equal spacing between decoys, which, he says, "gives them a single-file look that birds get wise to late in the season. It's even better to double anchor the line and put some curve in it. Then run the lines in several different directions so approaching birds can't see straight down a line of decoys."

line clips are strong and hold fast to the main line with a decoy attached even in rough weather. The next decoy is attached several feet down the line and so on. Long-line clips are large and can be handled with ease in cold weather and while wearing gloves. Long-line clips can be obtained from commercial fishing supply stores and some waterfowl supply catalogs.

Other methods are to tie loops in the main line, splice in metal rings, or attach short lines. In all cases, a large fishing-type snap-swivel is used to attach the decoys to the loop, ring, or line that comes off the main line. The swivel can be attached to the decoy's keel with a split ring or short length of line.

Improved clinch knot and slipknot.

According to Wade Bourne in *Decoys and Proven Method for Using Them* (Ducks Unlimited, 2000), good knots are paramount in securing lines to decoys and weights. He recommends the slipknot and the fisherman's improved clinch knot (used to connect a hook to monofilament line) for this purpose. If you are not using a swivel, a loop knot, keel knot, or any knot that forms a loop in the end is preferred.

Decoy Spreads

Now that we have picked out decoys and have rigged them with lines and anchors, the next order of business is the placement of the decoys—the decoy spread or set. Over the years, many time-tested decoy sets have been developed, including the fishhook pattern, V-pattern, and others. The number of decoys you use depends on the type of water you will be hunting, the level of competition from other hunters, the chronology of the migration, the species, and similar factors. In general, small water requires smaller and less elaborate decoy

A mix of diver and puddle duck decoys set in a classic V-pattern.

Ryan Falls, Arroyo City, Texas
"Fast Pickup"

Ryan Falls, who guides for redheads on the Laguna Madre, has come up with a fast way to bring in decoys. "We hunt in water that is less than 2 feet deep and use single-line decoys. I rig a 3-foot length of 400-pound monofilament, crimping it to the decoy on one end and to a 6- to 8-ounce smooth weight on the other. When bringing the decoys in, two guys take a 60-foot rope and walk to the outside of the spread. They then walk back in as they drag the rope around the decoys and pull them together in a tight group to the bank or against a blind. They are now gathered up and easy to drop into a bag, weight first. When you're ready to go the next day, dump the bag out and you will discover that few if any of the decoys are tangled."

spreads than does big water. Nothing, however, can replace time spent in the field observing how birds are using a particular area. Remember, you are trying to replicate how ducks sit on the water and interact with each other and the surrounding environment. In some cases, a random scattering of decoys works fine. More often, particularly when hunting diving and sea ducks in open water, knowing how to set decoys in a predetermined pattern will bring more ducks to the gun.

Shoreline Blind Sets

When setting decoys for shoreline blinds in a marsh, tidal area, or point on a lake or river, the direction of the wind is important. If possible, select a location where the wind blows away from or parallels the shoreline. This way the decoys can be set so the birds fly into the wind and toward the blind. Avoid shoreline locations where the wind is blowing toward the shooters. This wind direction requires ducks to fly over land for at least a short time as they approach the decoys. While puddle ducks generally have no problem flying over land, divers and sea ducks prefer to approach from open water. Puddle ducks often land short of the decoys; divers and sea ducks tend to land in the decoys or ahead of them.

If you are hunting a small wetland for divers, the number of decoys will vary from 12 to 36, depending on size of the wetland, use patterns, and how you are going to reach the area. If access is via boat, ATV, or some other vehicle, 24 decoys is about the right number on smaller waters and 36 on larger areas. Because there are generally puddle ducks in these areas, it's wise to use both mallard and scaup or other diver decoys. A basic set would be a dozen mallard decoys and 2 dozen diver blocks set in a horseshoe (Figure 1) or fishhook (Figure 2) pattern with a landing zone in front of the blind. Set the mallard decoys near the shore and the diver decoys trailing out into open water. The placement of the landing zone and tail of the fishhook or end of the horseshoe should be rotated to conform to the prevailing winds. Divers and sea ducks land into the wind and often start their approach at the tail of the fishhook or the farthest decoy and then fly up the line to the landing area. At least that's the plan! When making sets in smaller waters, decoys are generally rigged on single lines so they can be individually placed. That's also a good method if you have to pack them in; single-line, multiple-decoy rigs with heavy weights are cumbersome and impractical.

When rigging big-water sets for divers and sea ducks, larger numbers of decoys are used to mimic rafts and feeding flocks, as well as for their high visibility and drawing power. The best blind locations are points or fingers of land that jut into open water. Decoys can be rigged

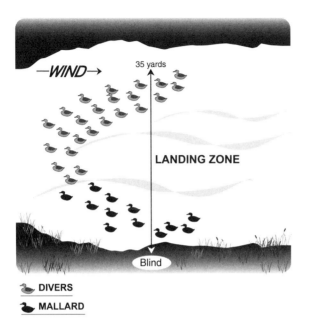

Figure 1

Basic horseshoe set for marsh or other small-water diver hunting using a combination of mallard and diver decoys rigged individually.

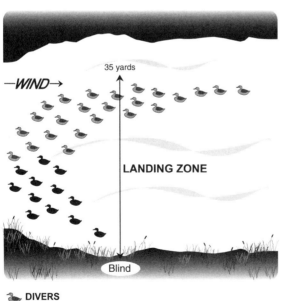

Figure 2

Fishhook set for marsh or other small-water diver hunting using a combination of mallard and diver decoys rigged individually.

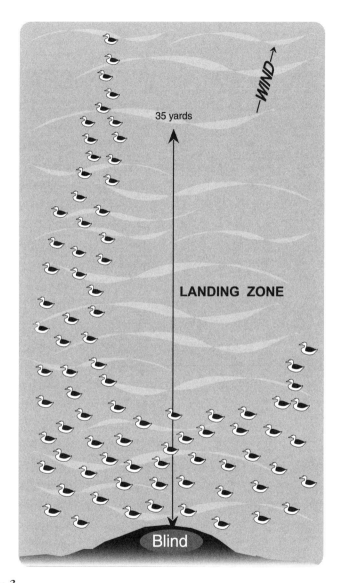

Figure 3

Fishhook or J spread set for big-water shoreline blinds using diver/sea duck decoys rigged on single-line, multiple-decoys rigs and decoys rigged individually.

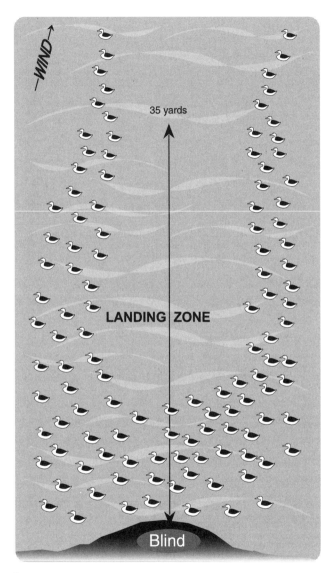

Figure 4

U spread set for big-water shoreline blinds using diver/sea duck decoys rigged on single-line, multiple-decoy rigs and decoys rigged individually.

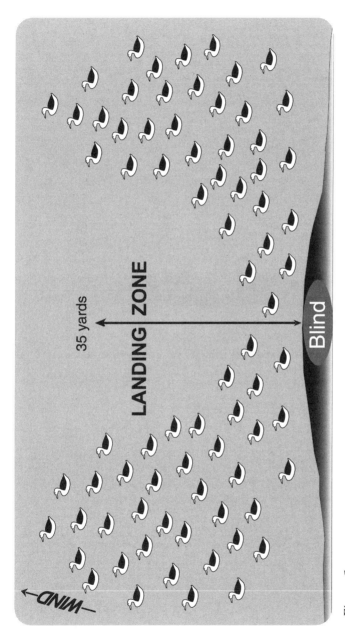

Figure 5

Double pod or two-rig set for big-water shoreline blinds using diver/sea duck decoys rigged on single-line, multiple-decoy rigs and decoys rigged individually.

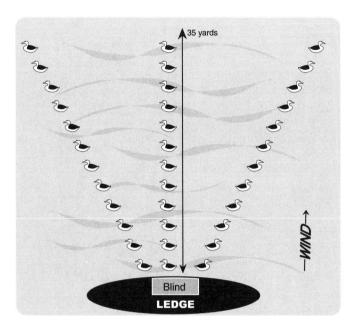

Figure 6

Spreader set for half-tide ledges using eider decoys on single-line, multiple-decoy rigs.

individually and then placed out one at a time, or rigged on single-line, multiple-decoys rigs of 6 to 18 decoys. Many seasoned diver hunters use a combination of the two techniques, using four or more strings with a dozen decoys each and another dozen decoys individually rigged. The single decoys are placed in front of the landing zone and on the edges and tail end of the spread to fill in the areas where a full string of a dozen decoys is not required. Common and time-tested setups are the fishhook or J spread (Figure 3) and horseshoe or U spread (Figure 4). If mallards or other dabblers are in the area, by all means put out a dozen or more mallard decoys and set them toward the shoreline in shallow water. The other option is often referred to as the double-pod spread or two-rig set (Figure 5). Here the decoys are

A big spread of decoys set in a fishhook pattern near an off-shore floating blind.

arranged in two separate groups with a large landing zone in the middle. If you add puddle duck decoys, place them at the bottom of the landing zone near the shoreline.

The spreader set (Figure 6) is popular in Maine when gunning eiders from half-tide ledges. The set utilizes three or four single-line, multiple-decoy rigs, each with 12 decoys. The lines are deployed from the base of the ledge to the open water. This pattern draws birds into the middle of the spread between the line of decoys.

Offshore and Floating Blind Sets

Unlike shoreline blinds that have land on at least one side, offshore and floating blinds are surrounded by water. This increases the area where decoys can be placed and, in many respects, makes putting out a decoy spread easier. With offshore locations, ducks can approach from any angle without crossing over land, and no matter what the wind direction is, you can adjust the decoys accordingly. The depth of water, wind direction, aspect and location of the nearest shoreline, and local flight patterns all affect the decoy set you use and how many decoys will be required.

When setting decoys for offshore blinds, most diver and sea duck hunters use at least 6 dozen decoys and some use 200 or more decoys. Setting out this many decoys makes the use of single-line, multiple-decoy rigs the most realistic method. Like shore blinds, if there are puddle ducks in the area, a dozen or more mallard, black duck, or other puddle duck decoys add realism to the spread and will draw in a few bonus dabblers.

One of the best sets for either a stake or floating blind is the modified fishhook or "big dipper" rig (Figure 7). This set uses 6–8 dozen diver decoys in long lines that funnel the diving ducks to a landing zone in front of the blind. Some 12–18 puddle duck decoys are placed behind the blind to draw the puddlers over the shooters. Another good offshore set for divers and sea ducks is the elongated double-pod spread (Figure 8) that incorporates two sets of decoys deployed in long lines with an opening in front of the blind.

Divers and sea ducks often feed along underwater ridges or reefs where there is bottom structure and a good food supply. In this case, the decoys can be set in long irregular lines with the blind in the middle of the set (Figure 9). Remember, diving and sea ducks have a tendency to land in the decoys, so it is usually productive to place the blind in the center of the spread where the long fingers of decoys guide the birds to your position.

Even though most decoys will be rigged on single-line, multiple-decoy rigs, it's wise to have a few decoys rigged on single lines to fill in the set or to place decoys at the very outside edge to help guide birds into the shooting zone. And don't forget flagging; it adds motion and realism to the spread, as do spinning-wing decoys.

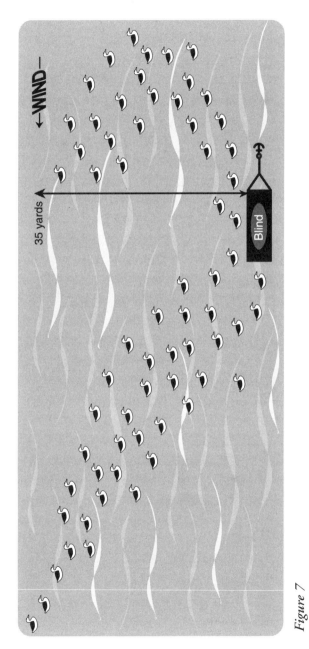

Figure 7

Modified fishhook or "big dipper" set for offshore or floating blinds using diver/sea duck decoys rigged on single-line, multiple-decoy rigs and decoys rigged individually.

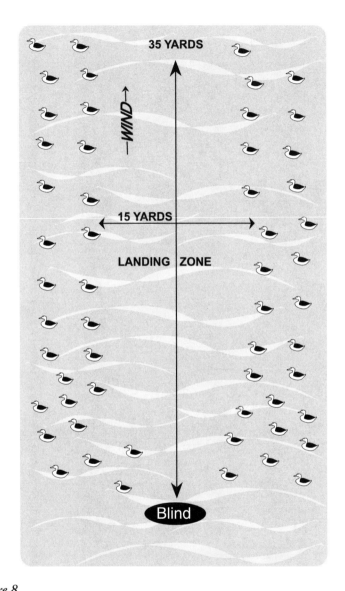

Figure 8

Elongated double pod set for offshore or floating blinds using diver/sea duck decoys rigged on single-line, multiple-decoy rigs.

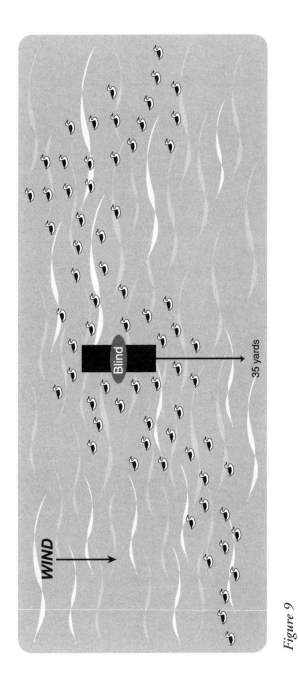

Figure 9

Irregular line set for offshore or floating blinds using diver/sea duck decoys rigged on single-line, multiple-decoy rigs and decoys rigged individually.

Capt. Ruben Perez, Cape Cod, Massachusetts
"Big-Rig Tactic"

Capt. Ruben Perez guides diving and sea duck hunters on Cape Cod. He advises: "Setting dozens of decoys to attract a flock of divers or sea ducks can take all day if the decoys are set with individual anchors. Experienced hunters use what's called the mother line, gang rig, or chain gang method. Regardless what you call it, it's the most effective method to deploy large numbers of decoys. The mother line is a 100-foot length of ¼-inch line with anchors on both ends. Salvaged window sash weights can be used as inexpensive anchors. The weights should be secured to an additional line, which will be attached to the main line; that length varies according to the water depth you are hunting. I use dog leash snaps on the ends of the anchor lines to make the rig flexible.

"Attaching decoys to the mother line can be done with long-line clips, commonly used in the commercial fishing industry. Marine supply vendors carry a variety of clips, but the larger ones with swivels are best. Tie a clip to every decoy with a short length of tarred line. Leave enough space between decoys so a retriever or your boat can navigate between them. At the start of your hunt, drop the anchor and play out line until you get to the main line. Then start attaching decoys with the snaps until reaching the end of the mother line. Attach the other decoy anchor line and play it out as you let the wind carry you into position. The whole set-up takes less time to deploy than to explain."

Capt. Jeff Coats, Bel Air, Maryland
"You Can't Flag Too Much"

After spending more than 90 days each season on Chesapeake Bay for the past eight years, Capt. Jeff Coats has found that next to a good spread of decoys, a black flag is the second most important tool when gunning for scoters. "With scoters you can never flag too much. A simple 2-foot by 2-foot square of black fabric on a dowel works fine. From a distance flagging definitely helps with the visibility of your decoy rig and draws in birds."

Layout Boat, Sink Box, and Sneak Boat Sets

Like offshore and floating blinds, layout boats and sink boxes are surrounded by water. Their position can be adjusted to conform to wind patterns, allowing ducks to land into the wind. Most sets customarily used for offshore and floating blinds can be used for layout boats and sink box hunting. A good set is the modified teardrop using at least 100 decoys (Figure 10). A teardrop is formed with the decoys. The tail of the teardrop is downwind of the layout or sink box and the large end of the teardrop upwind. Large open areas free of decoys are built into the spread to provide landing zones. If there are puddle ducks in the area, add a few mallard blocks and place them upwind of the layout boat or sink box and behind the shooter. This way puddle ducks will be drawn over or past the gunner while the divers and sea ducks will land below the boat or next to it.

While sneak boat shooting is the least practiced of the open-water hunting methods, a few hunters hold on to this time-tested style of waterfowling. A good decoy spread for sneak boat shooting is the square set (Figure 11), where several lines of decoys are set out with a shooting lane left open in the middle. Leave plenty of room between decoys—at least 6 feet—to give the feel of a relaxed flock; this should fool the birds into sitting long enough for you to make an approach in the sneak boat.

Calling Diving and Sea Ducks

Unlike calling for puddle ducks and geese, which has been elevated to a major league sport, calling for diving and sea ducks is in the bush leagues. The reason is simple—mallards, pintails, wigeon, black ducks, and other puddle ducks are vocal by nature and communicate by calling. Divers and sea ducks, on the other hand, call less frequently,

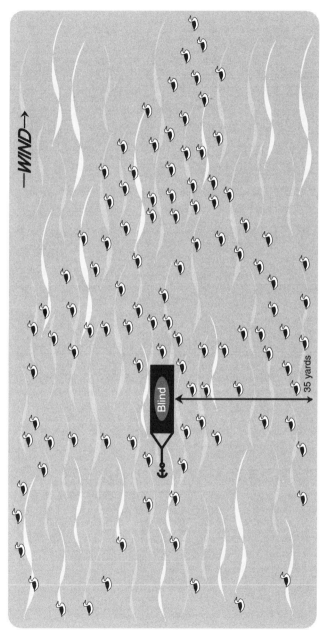

Figure 10

Modified teardrop set for layout or sink box rigs using diver/sea duck decoys rigged on single-line, multiple-decoy rigs and decoys rigged individually.

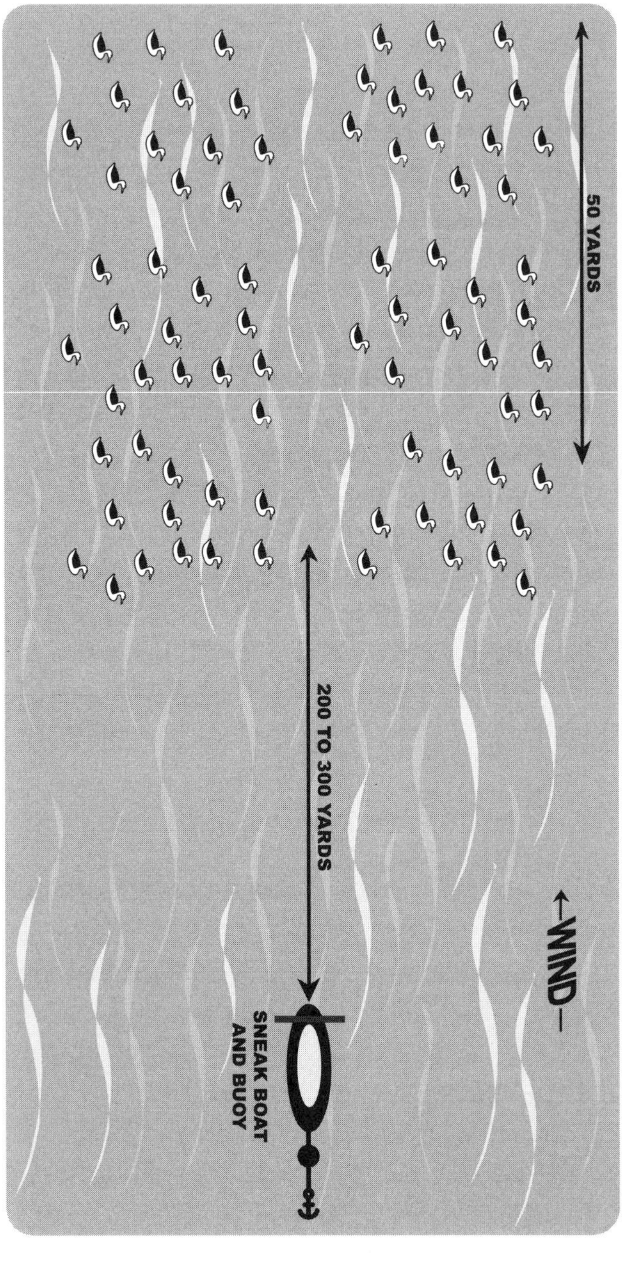

Figure 11

Square set for sneak boat rigs using diver/sea duck decoys rigged on single-line, multiple-decoy rigs.

Al Scavino, Richmond, California
"Use a Pintail Whistle for Bluebills"

"I have found that, at least in northern California where we hunt, a pintail or sprig whistle will call in bluebills," says veteran hunter Al Scavino. "Because our decoy spreads usually have twice as many pintail decoys as diving ducks decoys, the bluebills respond to the whistle and give us a good look. In open water, blow the whistle with plenty of volume."

A hunter blows a pintail whistle to attract diving ducks.

Tony Toye, Boscobel, Wisconsin
"Divers Can be Called"

When asked about calling diving ducks, Tony Toye, who guides on the Upper Mississippi River, says "As a flock of divers approaches for the first time I tend to be somewhat conservative with my calling. A few *brrr's* and soft quacks with my mallard call is usually all that's needed. If the flock does not decoy and continues past, I'll get aggressive. A loud mallard comeback call will often turn a flock of bluebills or cans around for another look. Once they've turned and are coming back, I decrease the volume a bit but continue to be aggressive. You'll be amazed how many more flocks of divers you can decoy when you call!"

Calling for divers can be effective in the right situations.

have a limited range of notes, and don't rely on calling as a primary form of communication.

While the selection is limited, calls made specifically for divers include the Bill Harper 450 Diving Duck Call manufactured by Lohman and the Diver Duck Call by Big River Game Calls. Additionally, a mallard call can be used, not to produce mallard sounds, but rather to produce a reedy *burr-burr-burr, purr-purr-purr,* or *prrrt-prrrt-prrrt* to mimic divers or sea ducks. The actual call

---

Capt. Ruben Perez, Cape Cod , Massachusetts
"Attracting Divers And Sea Ducks"

"One of waterfowling's most satisfying sights is watching a flock of puddle ducks bank and make their way into your rig due to your masterful calling," says Capt. Ruben Perez, who guides on Cape Cod. "Unfortunately, when gunning for divers and sea ducks, the use of a duck call is not very effective. Flagging with a small black flag, a l x l foot square attached to a short stick, can be just the trick to attract birds. The movement made by waving the flag back and forth will catch the ducks' attention long enough for them to see the decoys and come in. No flag in the layout? Your hat will do in a pinch. Or you can use your foot, as old-time diver hunters did years ago. It is said that they would move one foot at the divers, while reclining in the layout, as the ducks came in."

---

varies in pitch, depending on the species imitated. After they spend some time listening to diving ducks call in the field, most hunters find it easier to blow a duck call for divers than for mallards because there are fewer notes involved. If more than one person calls, the sound becomes more realistic; seldom does only one duck in a flock of divers do all the calling.

Generally, divers and sea ducks do not respond directly to the quacking calls of mallards or the whistle of pintails and wigeon. Still, some guides claim that a mallard highball call will attract scaup and canvasbacks to a spread of diver decoys. While calling divers using mallard notes is an area of debate, most seasoned diver hunters and guides agree that if there are puddle ducks in the area and you have puddle duck decoys in your spread, mallard calling can be effective as an indirect stimulus. It provides divers with a level of confidence, and while you are not actually calling the divers, it catches their attention and makes them feel more comfortable. The secret to using a mallard call for divers is to call sparingly and either call less aggressively or not call when birds are on their final approach and closing in on the decoys.

Does calling diving ducks work? The answer is: It depends. I have seen days when I am certain that calling makes the difference between two birds in the bag and a full limit. The next day, calling appears to do nothing. The inconsistency of effective calling for divers and sea ducks is the major reason why calling has not evolved as an integral part of this type of duck hunting like it has in puddle duck or goose hunting.

Chapter Five

DUCK BLINDS

Along with decoys and a shotgun, blinds are an integral part of duck hunting. Sure you can jump-shoot or shoot from a scull boat, but a blind is the focal point of most duck hunts. In the case of divers or sea ducks, the "blind" can be anything from wearing camouflage clothing and sitting still on a kelp-covered rock to an elaborate anchored floating boat blind or a pit blind that has bunks, a hot plate, and a portable toilet. The variety of blinds is endless and only restricted by your imagination, time, and pocketbook.

Duck blinds come in all shapes and sizes; this one doubles as a breakfast nook.

According to *Webster's Dictionary*, the word blind means "a place of concealment; esp: a concealing enclosure from which one may shoot game or observe wildlife." No matter what type of blind is used, the goal is to conceal the hunter from waterfowl. Blinds can be permanent—some have been in the same location for many years—or temporary and set in place for a day. They can be a fixed structure on pilings or timbers set in concrete, or they can be portable and easily moved by one individual. They can be as simplistic as a white sheet stretched between two poles on a snow-covered shoreline, or elaborate affairs with roll-back tops, camouflaged boat storage, card tables, stoves, and heaters. The more basic portable blinds are not as comfortable or user-friendly as elaborate permanent blinds, but they make up for it in mobility.

Diving and sea ducks are hunted in a variety of habitats, including marshes, lakes, reservoirs, tidal estuaries, and wind-swept coastlines. The one attribute these areas all share is water. Unlike puddle ducks and geese, which are sometimes hunted in dry grain fields and pastures, divers and sea ducks are always hunted over water. Blinds, therefore, are set on shorelines next to bodies of water or—in the case of silt blinds, boat blinds, layout boats, and sink boxes—in or over water. The most productive blinds are those placed in a location where the maximum number of birds will feed, roost, or fly by. The selection of a specific location for a permanent or temporary blind is often because the area "looks good" or because it is convenient. While these factors are important, nothing can match an area that is used on a daily basis by waterfowl for their core needs—food and security.

The blind should fit the location, and once constructed or set up, it should conceal the hunter thoroughly—from the sides, back, and top, if possible. Thought should also be given to decoy placement; select a location where the decoys can be deployed for maximum visibility. When camouflaging a fixed blind, paint all wooden surfaces inside and out with drab olive or marsh brown flat paint and cover the sides with chicken wire, woven wire, or camouflage netting. Finally, cover the exterior with local materials. Match the vegetation used on

© Bill Buckley

When possible fixed blinds should be camouflaged with the type of vegetation found in the local area.

the blind to the local area and use natural topography to blend the structure into the surroundings. If you're hunting next to tall reed beds, use reeds. If your blind will be next to a willow patch, use willow branches. Attach the vegetation to the netting or woven wire with cable ties, strong twist ties, or nylon cord. Avoid wire that can scratch, as well as light twine or string that will rot and break. Don't cut vegetation from the immediate area. You don't want to ruin the natural look of the immediate blind site. In some areas, blinds are covered with wood and painted to match the surroundings or are covered with vegetation, like palm fronds, brought in from other areas. While I prefer to use local vegetation, in some cases other materials are effective.

The position of the blind in relation to the prevailing winds and the direction of the sun is important, whether you are selecting a location for a permanent blind or setting up a portable blind for only one morning. Try to avoid setting up the blind with the sun directly in your face. The sun will illuminate your face like a neon sign. Moreover, looking into the sun is difficult and uncomfortable, and it also makes it hard to see the colors of the ducks that are approaching. It is better to set up with the sun at your back. Your face will be shaded and the birds will be in direct sunlight and their colors vivid. While not always possible, set the blind to face downwind so that the wind is blowing from behind you. If that is not possible, set up with a crosswind.

Where the size and type of construction allow, your blind should be comfortable and built to shield the hunters from the elements. That's not always possible. A hunter, for example, who is sitting on a half-tide ledge will be exposed to the elements. He will have to rely on his clothing for camouflage and comfort. But in most cases, when you build a blind, particularly an elaborate permanent structure, make sure it's comfortable and blocks the wind, rain, and snow. It should have a top, or at least a partially covered roof. Some hunters are concerned with the height or profile of a blind. If you are building a blind that is surrounded by vegetation, the rule of thumb is to build the blind no taller than the surrounding vegetation. This helps the blind fit the location. In open-water situations, height it not as important.

The longer you can stay in the field in comfort, the more ducks you will harvest. If it gets bone-chilling cold, bring a catalytic heater and hot coffee or put on an extra layer of clothes. How many times have you been freezing to death and headed back to the vehicle only to look over your shoulder to see a flock of scaup pitching into the spot you left? Staying in the field will keep those experiences to a minimum. And certainly there will be slow days when the weather is raw and the birds don't fly. This is when a comfortable blind is appreciated. As far as I'm concerned, it's better to suffer in comfort.

Stilt blinds (above and below) and other permanent blinds may be large and conspicuous, but diving and sea ducks grow accustomed to them over time and accept them as part of the landscape.

Permanent Blinds

Permanent blinds come in a variety of shapes and sizes—from the simple to the elaborate. They are built into the ground, along shorelines, on timbers buried in the mud, and on floating platforms. Because many permanent blinds are large and conspicuous, it is important to have them in place before the season starts so that ducks accept them as part of the landscape. Given enough time, it's amazing how ducks become accustomed to a structure. Years ago, I hunted redheads in Mexico from an old car body that had somehow ended up on a point in the Laguna Madre. The old, rusted-out sedan was half buried in the mud and someone had cut off the top. The first

time I saw it, redheads were feeding within 25 yards of the car. With decoys set and the right tidal level, the birds decoyed as if they were dropping into the best blind on the bay. I'm not advocating junked cars as blinds, but that "blind" demonstrates the importance of getting a permanent blind set up well before you intend to use it. Permanent objects become nearly invisible to waterfowl over time.

A duck boat delivers waterfowlers to their well-camouflaged floating blind.

The second consideration is to set or anchor your permanent blind in an area that birds use regularly. And once that location is found and the blind is built or anchored, don't overshoot it. Some guides never hunt the same blind two days in a row; others go back to the same blind day after day. If you hunt the same blind or area on a regular basis, be on the lookout for signs of overshooting—birds not decoying well, fewer birds near your blind, or more birds rafted in open water and sanctuary areas. Once waterfowl's use of an area drops off, let it rest to avoid running the birds out all together. On many duck clubs

Al Scavino, Richmond, California
"Floating Blind Placement"

Veteran diver hunter Al Scavino hunts in Grizzly Bay, east of San Francisco, where they set up a floating blind and leave it out all season. "We anchor our blinds with a swivel, so the blind rotates in a tight circle during changes in the tide and wind direction. Otherwise, the blind will uproot the decoys and ruin the spread. It is our intention to have one-half of our diving duck decoys on the lee of the floating blind. The prevailing winds are from the northwest and the storms from the south or southeast. The diving duck spread would be about 60 decoys, with 30 to the northwest and 30 to the southeast. This way, as the duck blind swings with the wind, one-half of the diving decoys are always in the lee of the blind. The balance of the spread are puddle duck decoys, and we put them out in the other two quadrants."

in California, members shoot only on Saturday, Sunday, and Wednesday. Some clubs shoot the same blind location only once a week. If your shooting drops off significantly and birds are still in the area, overshooting may be the culprit. Give the location some rest and the birds will likely return.

One of the main reasons hunters go to the trouble and expense of building permanent blinds is the comfort and convenience they provide. As you get older, the convenience of knowing where you are going to hunt, how to get there in the dark, and the comfort of the blind once you arrive can become more important than the dollars invested in building the structure. Because fixed blinds are in place prior to the season, once you arrive all the work has already been done.

There's no last minute need to brush up the blind, and the decoys may already be set or at least in the blind, ready to go.

Depending on the part of the country you hunt divers and sea ducks, there are generally preferred types of permanent or fixed blinds. In Humboldt Bay on the Pacific Coast, open-water stilt blinds are popular. They are generally constructed by driving piles or timbers in a rectangular or square pattern into the bottom of lakes, bays, or larger bodies of water. The piles are then stabilized by stringers placed on all four sides near the water level. A framework and solid floor are built on the lower stringers, and upper stringers are added to form a box. The sides between the two stringers are covered with wood or chicken wire and thatched with vegetation or netting. Some have partial tops while others have roll-back tops or no top at all.

When built in saltwater or freshwater locations where water levels fluctuate, the stringers are generally placed just above the high-water mark to avoid inundating the blind during high water. At low tide the blind many stand several feet above the water, with local conditions dictating when the shooting will be the most productive. Some stilt blinds are built to allow a boat to be brought alongside, and others allow the boat to be stored under the structure.

Floating blinds are similar to stilt blinds because they are generally set in open water, have camouflaged sides, and are designed for a boat to be brought alongside. In some cases, the boat is pulled into a camouflaged, anchored structure and secured to become the shooting platform. Floating blinds range from small blinds supported by Styrofoam floating docks to large blinds built on anchored barges or large pontoon boats. Formerly logs lashed together or empty oil drums were used, but in recent years easy-to-obtain Styrofoam dock sections have become the most popular base for floating blinds.

Floating blinds can be anchored to move up and down with fluctuating water levels and rigged to swing with the wind, allowing the

Though more popular in flooded agricultural fields and marshes, where dabbling ducks abound, pit blinds can be used to hunt divers and sea ducks near shorelines and other shallow-water areas.

decoys to be set based on the prevailing winds. While such blinds are considered fixed structures, they can be moved to a new location or towed to a storage location at the end of the season.

Pit blinds are holes dug into the ground that afford nearly complete concealment. Add a camouflaged or thatched top that swings or can be pushed out of the way, and you become invisible even in areas of limited vegetation. Pit blinds seem to be most popular in rice fields and marshes, where puddle ducks are the primary quarry, but there are some shoreline areas (particularly points on large lakes) where pits are used regularly for diver and sea duck gunning. Pits go beyond the low-profile approach to blinds and provide essentially no profile to ducks.

Pit blinds are typically round or rectangular structures built with concrete, welded sheet metal, or fiberglass and placed in a hole excavated by a backhoe. There is often a stabilizing device built into the blind or attached to it—extensions, cables with deadman weights, or such. These devices anchor the pit and keep it from popping out of the ground. Most pits eventually leak or fill with rainwater, and a sump pump and car battery can be rigged to pump the water out. Most

Jeff Petersen, Old Harbor, Alaska
"Use Cover Already in Place"

"**I** used to tell my clients to grab some driftwood and make a blind, but guys started building blinds on the shore and some of them looked like log cabins," says Jeff Petersen, who guides for sea ducks in Alaska. "To you a huge pile of driftwood may look natural, but to birds that fly past that point every day, it looks like trouble. Visualize yourself as a duck and try and see what it will see when it flies your way. Are you silhouetted against the skyline or water, or do the background and shadows hide you? The trick is to blend in and not move."

hunters, however, use a bucket and simply bail out the pit when necessary. If pit blinds are used in your area, talk to other hunters and find out which anchoring system they use and the type of blinds they prefer.

While open-water stilt blinds, pit blinds, and floating blinds are popular designs, the shoreline blind is a permanent structure familiar to virtually all duck hunters. Its design and construction is virtually the same as a stilt blind, but instead of building it in open water, it is located along a shoreline. Other permanent shoreline blinds are made of meticulously stacked rocks. Sometimes the blind is built to allow a boat to be pulled alongside or under it. At other locations, the boat is hidden down the shoreline. In some areas, access to fixed shoreline blinds is by foot or vehicle, which makes a boat unnecessary if you have a dog to retrieve and the water is shallow enough to wade. Otherwise a small pram or johnboat should be available to put out decoys and collect dead birds and cripples.

Like open-water stilt blinds, the shoreline blind can be built on pilings or post timbers set in the mud or dry ground along the edge of the water body. Then the basic box blind is built on the pilings or around the corner posts. A roof is important to shield hunters from the elements and is usually built on the back half of the blind with the front, or gunning portion, left open to allow hunters to stand up and shoot. Location has been discussed before, but the blind should be set so the ducks swing over water and toward the blind to the decoys as opposed to over land, which divers and sea ducks, in particular, avoid. Other blinds are built at the water's edge, and a floor is placed directly on the ground with the sides and top anchored to the floor. One of the best shoreline blinds I've seen was on low sand dunes at the edge of a huge lake in Michigan. It was a combination of a depression excavated in the sand, a solid wood floor, 4x4 corner posts, and walls covered with chicken wire and thatched with willow branches and reeds. Being part pit and part shoreline blind, it concealed the hunters, kept the wind and cold out, was low profile, and worked perfectly on the flocks of bluebills that were flying along the lakeshore. I've also seen decent fixed shoreline blinds where the sides and top where constructed of wood and the floor was either concrete, gravel, or—in one location— knee-deep mud. I guess it depends on your expected comfort level.

If a permanent blind will be used for several years, it's wise to cultivate or plant native vegetation near the blind. In a few years you'll have natural camouflage growing around your blind. It will be invisible to ducks, and the amount of work required each year to camouflage the blind will diminish.

No matter what type of permanent blind you build, it is a good idea to build notches or a place to safely lean your shotgun where it won't fall over while you are waiting for birds to decoy. A shelf where you can set your shells, a coffee thermos, and a fire extinguisher are also helpful.

Portable Blinds

Portable or temporary blinds are the choice of many freelance hunters. Their greatest advantage is they allow the hunter to take his concealment with him. This flexibility allows mobility, so changing conditions can work for you rather than against you. If the birds move to a new feeding or roosting area, you can follow. If the birds are pushed from one area to another due to excessive hunting pressure, you can go to the new area even if it's a pond that is small and difficult to reach. The disadvantages are that portable blinds are not as comfortable as permanent blinds, and they do not protect hunters from the elements as thoroughly. Additionally, many hunters do not have the physical stamina or ability to carry a portable blind around or even hike in waders to areas where natural vegetation can be used as the blind.

Like permanent blinds, the purpose of a portable blind is concealment. It must prevent ducks from seeing the hunter, provide a mini-

Proper camouflage clothing can help break up your outline and make you invisible to ducks, even in the absence of a blind or other cover.

mum level of protection from the weather, and provide a bit of comfort even if the blind amounts to nothing more than sitting behind a camouflage netting on a plastic bucket. Above all, the portable blind must be a structure that can be moved easily or, in the case of using natural vegetation, be able to hide the hunter. I'm a firm believer than hunters should wear camouflage clothing and use some method of breaking up their outline. I also believe it's not necessary to have a solid wall of vegetation between the hunter and the ducks.

Among the many types of portable blinds, the use of natural cover and camouflage clothing is the simplest. With this method you don't have to carry a blind around and set it up, worrying that the wind might blow it over or that the camouflage pattern doesn't match the local vegetation. When using natural cover, you can build a blind by stacking driftwood on a point, hiding in a jumble of rocks, or standing in two feet of water in tall vegetation or shoreline brush. The choices are endless. Divers and sea ducks are often easier to fool than puddle ducks, and remaining motionless in a minimal blind is often all that's required. At other times, divers and sea ducks can be difficult to decoy and every bit as wary as puddle ducks, particularly late in the season.

The most basic portable blind beyond the use of natural vegetation is the use of grass mats, netting, mesh, or camouflage material. These products are sold by outdoor catalog companies like Cabela's and Herter's, and provide a screen that breaks up your outline and prevents ducks from seeing you. The material can be attached to stakes or tree branches set in the mud, draped between two bushes, or used to cover you and a small boat. An effective blind can also be made with a roll of chicken wire attached to several stakes with reeds or bulrush woven through the wire.

There are also a number of commercially made portable blinds that are built around an aluminum frame covered by camouflage-pattern canvas. Many are collapsible, while others are put together once a hunting location has been selected. Some are built to resemble tree stumps and can be set along the water's edge or in shallow water.

In recent years, layout field blinds like the Final Approach Eliminator Blind and Avery Finisher Blind have become popular with goose and duck hunters who do most of their gunning in grain fields and pastures. Most have spring-loaded lids or panels that fold in to close the top and spring open when the shooter sits up to fire. They are relatively comfortable and have built-in back and head rests. These same layout blinds can be effective on diving and sea ducks when set up along the edge of a lake or estuary where there is minimal vegetation. I've seen them smeared with mud and set up on a bare mud flat next to a tidal gut in an area where it would normally be impossible to hide.

Capt. Ruben Perez, Cape Cod, Massachusetts
"Layout Boat Anchoring"

Capt. Ruben Perez hunts the Massachusetts coast from Boston to Cape Cod and finds traditional layout hunting with a low-profile pumpkinseed-style boat one of waterfowling's most exiting methods. "After finding a productive spot where birds have been feeding or resting," he advises, "the next item of business is to anchor the layout. The layout is anchored fore and aft to keep it from swinging. The use of a large Danforth-style anchor at the head of the rig keeps it stationary against the wind and tide. A 12-pound mushroom-style anchor can be used for the stern anchor. Now the layout's position can be regulated to adjust for a tide or wind change, allowing you to keep the boat safely near your decoy rig. All you need to do now is get ready for close, in-your-face decoying action."

Boat Blinds

Not only are boats used for transportation to the hunting area, they are commonly used as a portable blind. The greatest advantage of a boat blind is its mobility. If the birds change their use patterns, you can go to the birds. And as long as there is water, you can anchor this shooting platform near marsh vegetation, in open water, or along a rocky shoreline.

Some are grandiose, like the 20-foot boat pushed by a 90-horsepower outboard that Tony Toye uses on the Upper Mississippi River in Wisconsin. During the season, Toye spends virtually every day on the water hunting ducks. He has developed a boat that serves his needs

Capt. Jeff Coats, Bel Air, Maryland
"Open-Water Anchoring"

According to Capt. Jeff Coats, "Because you need to move fast when chasing downed birds, I place a float on the end of my boat anchor line. When the time comes, I simply cast off the line and head for the crippled bird. When I return to the float I hook it to the boat and I'm back in position to shoot without resetting the anchor."

A duck boat that might double as a fishing boat come summer.

and provides his clients with a mobile and comfortable shooting platform This single-purpose, custom-made boat has a flat-bottomed hull and grass-covered panels that can be raised and lowered to hide hunters who are seated under a roof that covers half the boat. Wisconsin state law requires that boats be anchored in emergent vegetation. Once that takes place, the boat-turned-blind is surrounded by 120 decoys. While the hunters are waiting for the action to begin, Toye fires up a propane stove and soon the aroma of hot coffee and bacon fills the air.

Not all boats are as fancy as Toye's. Many hunters prefer 12- to 16-foot boats that during the summer are used to take the kids fishing. In

A pop-up boat blind provides excellent concealment from divers and sea ducks.

the fall, these boats make the transformation to a portable blind by the addition of a prefabricated boat blind, like the models manufactured by Avery Outdoor Products and Pop-Up Boat Blinds. Most commercially made boat blinds are designed to collapse out of the way when the boat is underway. Once you reach the shooting area, the blind is set up. These products provide excellent concealment, are relatively light, and do not affect the performance of the boat. They do, however, cost $500–$800 and take some time to install. Once the duck season is over, the blind portion is removed and stored until next year and the craft is transformed back to a fishing boat.

Long before there were commercially made blinds to attach to your boat, duck hunters made their own boat blinds. Some were the

165

same basic design used today for commercial collapsible boat blinds made of camouflage cloth over a frame of wood or metal. Others were rigid structures that could be lifted off the boat. A few were dedicated hunting boats with a permanent blind affixed to the hull. Some still use camouflage cloth or canvas to conceal the hunter while others use netting, burlap, grass mats, natural vegetation, painted plywood, or a combination of materials. I've seen 16-foot fiberglass boats with wooden sides painted black and anchored in Pamlico Sound in North Carolina, and I have hunted from a 25-foot fishing boat covered with a huge camouflage net anchored off Cape May, New Jersey. Both setups provided concealment, were anchored in the flight path of passing sea ducks—and the birds decoyed as if the blinds didn't exist. The moral of the story is this: If the type of boat blind you use is effective and works, don't knock it.

When building your own blind, consider the weight and don't build the blind so it makes the boat unstable and top-heavy. Remember, you'll have to move the boat to your hunting area before it can be transformed into a blind. Keep safety in mind when building the blind and running the boat.

Several companies have designed and built boats specifically for waterfowl hunting. These modern-day factory-made boats were not the first to be designed for duck hunting. The Barnegat Bay sneak boat was made for a specific type of duck hunting. Today's duck boats are more seaworthy, foam-filled, and unsinkable. And they are built for a wide range of hunting scenarios and conditions. A popular model is The Duck Boat, or TDB. It has sides that slope inward to provide concealment and brackets to add grass mats or other upright camouflage to convert it to a floating blind. Additionally, there are gun racks and storage areas for decoys. It is available in 14-, 17-, and 21-foot models and can handle big outboards. The Duck Wrangler comes in 14-, 15-, 17-, and 21-foot models. The 17- and 21-footers are heavy and are not designed for use in shallow water, but they perform well in big-water situations.

Low in profile, a layout boat painted in drab colors is a blind unto itself.

Layout boats are boat blinds, and scull boats can be converted to boat blinds. Coffin blinds are plastic or fiberglass tubs that hunters lie in to ambush ducks. An Aqua Pod is part kayak and part canoe, while Poke Boats and canoes are small, narrow craft that can be propelled by oars, paddles, or a small outboard. All of these boats are low-profile and can be used as boat blinds, provided they are properly camouflaged and set in the proper location. Diving and sea duck hunters find these single-man boat blinds most effective in marshy areas or locations where the cover is low and other types of blinds may be too conspicuous. In the right location, they are deadly.

Regardless of the type of boat blind you use, consider the direction of the wind when setting up and use two anchors to hold the boat in place. Where the water depth allows, some hunters use poles driven into the mud on each side of the boat to reduce the rocking caused by hunters rising to shoot. The lower the center of gravity you can maintain, the more stable the boat (shooting platform) will be. The boat will be more stable if you can stand on the floor and shoot rather than standing on the seats or a board placed across the seats.

Chapter Six

SCOUTING

Scouting and gathering information are more important than most hunters realize. I've heard it said that 10 percent of the hunters bag 90 percent of the game. This may be an exaggeration, but it's true that the distribution of the harvest,

Savvy waterfowlers observe flying ducks and try to pinpoint their destination.

whether it is deer or ducks, is not evenly divided among the participants. I believe that the individuals who are successful most of the time are the hunters who thoroughly scout and record information on a regular basis. Guides are in the field daily, and scouting and intelligence gathering are important parts of their operation because their livelihood depends on it. Hunters can take a lesson from guides and do the best scouting job they can given their individual time constraints.

A good example of the benefits of scouting took place several years ago in Texas. I was on my way to a quail hunt in Mexico. I decided to go a couple of days early and fish on the Laguna Madre before heading south. The first morning while fishing the flats for redfish, we noticed several flocks of birds lifting off the Laguna and heading inland. At first we thought they were shorebirds, but as we moved the boat closer, it became apparent they were redheads. The Texas duck season was still a week away, and according to my buddy it was the first time that fall he had seen redheads in this area.

The next day, between catching redfish, we watched as the ducks lifted off the Laguna and headed inland. Eventually we stopped fishing and did our best to follow the flights. It took 45 minutes to determine where the birds were heading. Soon there was a two-way flight of redheads—some were heading toward the shore, while others were returning to the Laguna. Back at my buddy's house, we made a few phone calls to local duck hunters, trying to determine specifically where the birds were going. None of them had a clue. We also called a biologist and asked him if he knew. He didn't know the location of the birds but did point out that it was common for redheads and other ducks to fly inland to freshwater ponds. This particular year had been very dry and the salt content of the Laguna was higher than normal. Ducks have salt glands that allow them to drink salt water and then excrete excess salt through their nasal glands. Since the salinity was higher than normal, their salt glands were working overtime and their reliance on fresh water had increased.

© Ron Spomer

Binoculars are an indispensable aid for viewing distant ducks.

The next morning we jumped in the vehicle and went to the area we thought the birds were using. It took more than an hour of searching, including standing on the roof of the pickup with binoculars, but we finally located a 25-acre freshwater pond with at least 5,000 red-heads and a few pintails and teal. As luck would have it, my buddy knew the family that owned the property. We stopped by the owner's house and were given permission to hunt the following weekend.

I went on my quail hunt in Mexico and was back in time for opening day. We arrived at the pond while it was still dark and tossed out 2 dozen redhead decoys and a dozen pintail blocks. Even before the sun peaked above the horizon, the first flock of redheads came barreling in at full speed, putting on the brakes at the last minute to land. We both picked out a drake and fired. Two redheads went cartwheeling across the pond in a spray of feathers. Not five min-utes later, with the crimson red glow of dawn as a backdrop, a hundred redheads came in hard, banked right, and dropped their feet to land. My partner missed his first shot and then pulled the rug out from under a bird on his second shot. I've watched plenty of divers come into decoys, but I was so awestruck with the sound and sight of so many birds on us

A good time to scout is right after a morning hunt, gathering intelligence for the next day and beyond.

at once, I didn't fire a shot. Soon another flock arrived and I came to my senses and bagged my second redhead to fill out our limit on that species. We added a couple of bonus teal and pintails to the bag, and I put my shotgun away and grabbed my camera. To this day, the photos

---

Joe Lucey, Waldo, Maine
"Nothing Can Replace Good Scouting"

Accoring to Joey Lucey, who guides along the coast of Maine, "Many variables come into play when deciding where to set your decoys. Scouting is vital to determine where the birds want to go naturally at all tide phases and various wind speeds and directions. This may sound simplistic, but it is important. While there are many traditional feeding and resting areas, these change daily and sometimes hourly, so it's important to stay on top of things with good scouting."

I took that morning are the best flying redhead images I have in my photo files.

The next year I called my buddy, who said only a handful of redheads were using the pond. I also called the biologist, and he said that because rainfall had been plentiful, the salinity in the Laguna was actually below normal levels. The water of the Laguna was not as salty

---

Ernie Spaulding, Jonesboro, Maine
"Get Friendly with the Locals"

"Even though it seems like I'm on the water all the time," says Ernie Spaulding, who guides on Pleasant Bay, Maine, "I don't cover nearly as much water as most of the local fishermen. I talk to these guys on a regular basis and they have become very helpful in letting me know where the ducks are working. Sometimes they even give me a call when they see a new concentration of birds."

---

as it had been the year before. This explained the lack of redheads on the pond. The birds' salt glands were keeping up with their salt intake. I've checked the pond several times since, and redheads use it only periodically.

This story points out that by putting in time, keeping your eyes open, gathering intelligence (in this case via phone calls), and scouting (we used both a boat and vehicle) you can take advantage of a good thing when it happens. While this particular incident came as a complete surprise, scouting before you leave home and taking advantage of the situation once you arrive are both critical in achieving success.

Direct scouting entails observing the birds directly, on the water or in the air.

There are really two methods of scouting or information gathering —direct and indirect. In the Laguna Madre scenario we used both. The direct scouting was the time spent in the boat watching the birds, and the next day in the vehicle looking for them. We used binoculars combined with good observation skills that picked up the first flock in the distance. The indirect method we used was the telephone calls we made

A flock of canvasbacks about to land.

to locate the landowner and talk with the biologist and other duck hunters, as well as the visit to the landowner's house to ask permission.

Nothing can beat the information gained by networking or communicating with people who share your interests. You never know when an important bit of information may present itself. As part of the networking strategy, attend DU dinners to meet people, share stories, and pick up information. Get involved with local sportsman's groups, rod and gun clubs, sporting clays leagues, and dog trials. Attend sportsmen's shows. Join state waterfowl associations and volunteer for cleanup days and projects with fish and game departments and wildlife refuges. The people you meet will share your interests, and if you cultivate these relationships, they will pay dividends. It could mean finding a new hunting location or keeping abreast of the latest shotgun loads or hunting equipment. If you can find even a few hunters, guides, or landowners who are willing to provide reliable information or help out in some way, you will be way ahead of the game. If you expect this information to keep coming, plan to reciprocate by freely providing information from your area. If a landowner grants permission to hunt, stop by later with a bottle of wine or other small gift that says thanks. If a guide or hunter is particularly helpful, send him or her a duck call, book, or other token of appreciation.

Cellular telephones are valuable not only for safety but to communicate with other hunters and information sources. Cellular coverage has increased in recent years, and more areas now have good coverage. I've literally picked up my decoy spread and moved my boat several miles based on a cell phone call from one of my buddies.

Another excellent tool for gathering information is the Internet. There are a number of chat rooms where you can communicate with other duck hunters, including Duck Hunters' Refuge (www.duck-hunter.net) and The Duck Hunter's Boat Page (www.duckboats.net). By asking questions you can often determine migration timing, where the birds are at any given moment, the type of decoys and calls that are working, and other pertinent information. These chat rooms produce a wealth of information for the expert and novice duck hunter alike.

Boyd King, Tofield, Alberta
"Don't Forget Scouting"

According to Boyd King, who guides waterfowl hunters in Alberta, "As with any hunting, success is largely dependent on scouting. Diver hunting is no different. Do yourself a favor and spend the time to figure out where the birds are feeding and roosting. If you find a spot on a point or in a reed bed along the flight path and between the feeding and roosting areas, you will have significantly increased your chances of success. This single factor may well be more important than decoys, decoy sets, and the like. Once you have birds passing by your decoys, you can then do the fine-tuning to get them in range."

The Weather Channel (www.weather.com) is well known to many Americans, including duck hunters. Enter any zip code or city in the country and a ten-day forecast will pop-up. Look for storm fronts moving into the area, cold snaps, and other weather patterns that trigger duck movements, both local and migratory.

All governmental agencies, including the U.S. Fish and Wildlife Service (www.fws.gov), have Web sites that are valuable in obtaining regulations, harvest information, breeding and wintering waterfowl population data, and other information. Many national wildlife refuges have Web sites, as well, and post weekly

Bluebills rafting and resting midday will likely move to feeding areas in the evening and morning hours.

waterfowl counts, harvest data, and public hunting information. State game departments and departments of natural resources (DNRs) all have Web sites that provide information on current regulations and public hunting areas. They can be accessed via a Web site (www.fishandwildlife.org) that has a link to all fifty states. The U.S. Army Corps of Engineers (www.usace.army.mil) controls water levels and releases on many impoundments and flood control projects throughout the United States, while the Bureau of Reclamation (www.usbr.gov) deals with water issues in the West. Many states also have waterfowl associations that can prove information, and the Ducks Unlimited Web site (www.ducks.org) provides data on current trends in waterfowl conservation and other information of interest.

Maps will aid in the information-gathering phase prior to a trip and during your scouting forays. Road maps indicate what route to take; topographic maps provide details on terrain; and aerial maps can pinpoint an access site or potential shoreline blind location. When hunting public and even private land, it's important to know exactly where you are to avoid trespass problems. Topographic maps are available from the U.S. Geological Survey Distribution Center (303-202-4700; www.usgs.gov). If you hunt on public lands, maps are available (some free, others for a small fee) from the agency that administers the property. Some state fish and wildlife agencies offer sportsmen's atlases or maps that show public hunting areas, boat ramps, and other sites on state-administered lands. River charts can be purchased from the U.S. Army Corps of Engineers, and lake maps can be obtained from the Bureau of Reclamation.

Private companies also offer maps. An excellent set of maps has been compiled by DeLorme (207-846-7000; www.delorme.com), and maps are available for most states as an atlas and gazetteer. Another private company that offers maps is Maptech (888-839-5551 or 978-792-1198; www.maptech.com). They offer an atlas, and free maps can be downloaded from their Web site. Aerial photo maps are available free and can be downloaded from www.TerraServer.com.

If you are traveling to hunt, make sure ducks will be in the area when you arrive. If it's a migration or staging area, make sure the birds have arrived but haven't headed south yet. On the wintering grounds, be sure they are present when you show up. These movements generally occur in set patterns. The first scaup arrive by early October at Lake of the Woods on the Minnesota-Ontario border; numbers peak between October 10 and 25; and most of them have departed by November. Similarly, the first canvasbacks arrive in Chesapeake Bay to spend the winter by Thanksgiving and stick around until March. Weather, hunting pressure, food availability, and other factors can alter migration patterns and bird movements. Therefore, reliable and up-to-date information is invaluable and may save you from disappointment.

To determine the chronology of the migration and other local conditions, water levels in rivers and lakes, tides, and such, contact guides, fish and game departments or DNRs, other state or federal agencies, sporting goods stores, and anyone else who might be able to provide information. It's foolish to spend time, energy, and money only to get there and find no birds are present. Do your homework and you will be rewarded.

Even hunters who shoot near their home need to scout. A sudden release of water may lower the water in a reservoir and expose points that are ideal for diver sets. A release from a dam may raise the water level in the river corridor below and inundate some of your favorite hunting areas. By keeping abreast of local conditions you can alter your hunting scenario to fit the current circumstances. Ducks respond quickly to changing conditions and literally can be in one place today and fifty miles away tomorrow. If you keep up with local movements, you will kill ducks.

Scouting and intelligence gathering should become a vital part of your hunt planning. With the help of the Internet, along with good old-fashioned conversations, you will be more focused and better able to find where the ducks are.

Chapter Seven

SHOTGUNS AND LOADS

Remington 1100 Classic Field

Until the late 1880s, the shotguns in use were hinge-action single-barrel or double-barrel side-by-sides in both hammer and hammerless models. Winchester was the first to market repeating shotguns, in 1887, and came out with the lever-action in 10-gauge and 12-gauge. In 1893, Winchester developed the first pump shotgun, and by the turn of the century, Browning unveiled the first semi-automatic, the Auto-5. In addition to lever-action, pump, semi-auto (also referred to as an autoloader), and hinge-action shotguns, other actions include bolt action, two-shot autoloaders, and double rifle–shotgun combinations.

The most popular actions today for waterfowling are the semi-auto, pump, and double-barrel designs. These repeating shotguns deliver at least two shots, and in pumps and semi-autos several shots, in quick succession as the shooter keeps his eye trained on the target. Every hunter has his or her own preference, and there are equally valid arguments for each type of gun. Like many things in shooting, it comes down to personal preference.

Gauges and loads for waterfowling can be confusing, compounded by the requirement that steel shot or other nontoxic shot be used for waterfowl hunting.

Shotgun Actions

When a young person first starts hunting, price is often the determining factor in the choice of shotguns, as is the circumstance. Many young hunters grow up with hand-me-down single-barrel shotguns. Others, like me, purchased a bolt-action shotgun back in the early 1960s because it was inexpensive. Mine lasted one season, and I made the quantum leap in price and quality to a Remington 870 pump. About fifteen years ago I switched to an over-under, and now use a double gun for all my shooting. Unless you are a seasoned shooter who already knows what action you prefer, use several action types before deciding on a shotgun to purchase. If you shoot a pump, try borrowing a semi-auto or a double gun and give it a try. Sporting clays ranges often have shotguns for rent, and all three popular actions are generally available for a test drive.

With semi-auto shotguns, once the first shell is fired, it's automatically ejected and the next round is automatically fed from the magazine to the chamber. All the shooter has to do is pull the trigger. The action is either gas-powered (gases generated by the expansion of the powder ignition) or recoil-powered (energy from the recoil itself). In both cases, the shooter can fire multiple shots as fast as he can pull the trigger. Many people like semi-autos over pumps because there is no slide to pull back, and compared to double guns there is a third shot available. Pumps and autoloaders are capable of holding more than three shells, but when used for migratory waterfowl, federal regulations require that they be plugged so the guns are capable of holding no more than three shells.

Semi-autos are often the choice of hunters who are concerned with recoil. Autoloaders, particularly gas-operated models, have less recoil than fixed-bolt shotguns because part of the energy released when a shell is fired is used to operate the ejection and loading mechanisms.

As a result, less recoil is transferred to the shoulder of the shooter. Gas-operated models have the highest recoil reducing characteristics. The downside to autoloaders, compared to pumps or double guns, is the maintenance required. In order to keep them in top working order, the guns must be thoroughly cleaned on a regular basis.

Ithaca Storm 12-Gauge Pump

A pump, or slide-action, shotgun is operated by pulling a slide back to eject the spent round and then moving the slide forward to load a shell and lock the bolt in place for firing. The round can then be fired by pulling the trigger, or the live round can be ejected by depressing a button on the bottom of the action. Pump-action shotguns are less expensive than semi-autos or double-barrel guns, and are extremely reliable in the field. The old Remington 870 I used for nearly two decades was dropped in the mud, immersed in salt water, and performed flawlessly with a minimum amount of cleaning and maintenance.

The major concern of shooters unfamiliar with a pumpgun is the requirement that the slide be "pumped" back and forth to operate the action. Granted, this takes some practice, but a pump in the hands of a seasoned shooter can be operated as quickly and effectively as an autoloader. Shooters who are accustomed to autoloaders will notice more recoil when using a pumpgun. Some hunters swear by pumps for waterfowling even though they can afford the best autoloader on the market.

Break-action or hinge-action shotguns come in both single-barrel and double-barrel models, and in doubles the configuration can be either side-by-side or over-under. A lever on the back of the receiver "breaks" the shotgun open, and shells are manually loaded. The gun is closed, and you're ready to pull the trigger. To remove spent shells, the

Beretta Onyx Pro Series Over-Under

action is opened and the shells are manually removed from the chambers or ejected with automatic ejectors. Due to their limitation of holding just one shell, very few single-barrel shotguns are used for waterfowl hunting.

The primary advantage of break-action shotguns is their reliability. Compared to semi-autos, and even pumps, there are very few moving parts. Additionally, with two separate barrels, different chokes can be used. Before the advent of steel shot and screw-in chokes, many waterfowl hunters used doubles choked modified and full. The modified barrel was used for incoming birds over the decoys and the full as the bird was flying away and farther from the shooter. The downside is more recoil, particularly with heavy loads, and the double's limitation of only two rounds. Many hunters use their third shot to anchor cripples more frequently than shooting at three targets. The double has to be reloaded in order to fire more than two shells. Finally, double-barrel shotguns, even the low-end models, are more expensive than semi-autos or pumps. Having said that, there are many hunters who wouldn't trade their double guns for any firearm, and take even the most expensive doubles into the marshes and saltwater estuaries. Just make sure you clean that fine double the second you are out of the field.

Gauges, Loads, and Chokes

While nontoxic shot is now manufactured for all shotgun gauges, the best waterfowl loads have been developed for 10-, 12-, and 20-gauges. The 28-gauge and .410 are too small for most waterfowl hunting, particularly for divers and sea ducks, and the 16-gauge is the least popular gauge in the United States. The 10-gauge is used by a few waterfowl hunters who pass-shoot at long ranges or want plenty of knockdown power. The 20-gauge is used by seasoned duck hunters and young shooters, particularly when ducks are in close over decoys. But day in and day out, some 90 percent of today's duck hunters use a 12-gauge. If we restrict that to hunters who pursue primarily diving and sea ducks, it's probably closer to 99 percent.

Premium steel-shot loads from Kent Cartridge.

It should come as no surprise, then, that the greatest variety of shells and loads are available in 12-gauge. Nontoxic loads for 12-gauge come in 2¾-, 3-, and 3½-inch shell lengths; 10-gauge ammo comes in 3½-inch length only. In 20-gauge, both 2-¾- and 3-inch nontoxic shot shells are widely available.

The larger the gauge and the longer the shell, the more shot it can hold. For example, a 3½-inch magnum (maximum) load in 10-gauge might hold 1¾ ounces of steel shot. A similar magnum load in a 3-inch, 12-gauge will hold 1½ ounces, and a 2¾-inch, 20-gauge magnum load may hold only 1 ounce of shot. The shell with the most shot delivered with the most energy effectively delivers the greatest knockdown power. Without getting into shotgun shell ballistics, a 10-gauge delivers more shot and knockdown power on target than a 20-gauge. The 12-gauge seems to be the middle ground and delivers plenty of knockdown power, yet it doesn't produce heavy recoil like a 10-gauge and delivers more shot and punch than a 20.

Blake LaRue, Uyak Bay, Alaska
"Sea Ducks Are Tough"

"Sea ducks are big, strong birds that require hard-hitting loads for clean kills," says Blake LaRue, a guide on Kodiak Island. "I use big shot and fast steel, or even better, other non-toxic shot. Even though we shoot decoying birds, the strong diving and swimming ability of sea ducks enables them to outdistance a dog quickly. Therefore, it's important to shoot cripples the second they hit the water. 'I can't believe how tough these birds are' is a phrase I hear from my hunters all the time."

The choice of shot size and load is as important as the gauge. Most loads designed specifically for waterfowl hunting are high velocity and have medium to heavy shot loads delivered with enough energy to consistently kill waterfowl. When using steel, waterfowl hunters need shot sizes larger than what was customary for lead shot. This is necessary to overcome the lighter weight and density of steel compared to lead. When hunting ducks over decoys, No. 5 or No. 6 lead shot—and occasionally No. 4—was recommended. With steel in the same shooting scenario, I use No. 3s or No. 2s. A general rule when purchasing loads for diver and sea duck hunting is to use heavier loads and larger shot for long shots and lighter loads and smaller shot sizes for close-in shooting. For

Remington Nitro-Steel Magnum shells.

example, many seasoned eider shooters who hunt these big birds late in the season use 12-gauge shotguns and 3½-inch shells loaded with magnum BB or No. 1 steel loads. Earlier in the season, when the birds decoy in close and their heavy winter plumage is less well developed, the same shooters use 3-inch, 12-gauge magnum shells and No. 1 or No. 2 shot. I'm a firm believer in using the load that will do the job without resorting to more firepower than necessary. That way, it's easier on your shoulder and your pocketbook. Take a look at the price of a magnum 10-gauge load in 3½-inch shells compared to the widely accepted 3-inch, 12-gauge loads. Most diver and sea duck hunters select 12-gauge magnum loads with 1⅜ or 1½ ounces of No. 1, No. 2, and occasionally BB steel shot.

The nontoxic alternatives to steel shot have pellets made of bismuth, tungsten, nickel, iron, and combinations of these metals. These loads behave much like lead, retain energy at longer distances than steel, and deliver a uniform shot pattern. Many hunters swear by the alternatives to steel and claim they outperform steel significantly, particularly when shooting beyond 35 yards. Additionally, fewer birds are crippled at any distance. Steel, on the other hand, generally has higher muzzle velocity that gets the shot to the target quicker than lead, making many hunters better shots, particularly when shooting between 20 and 35 yards. Very few hunters miss birds by shooting in front of

Federal's Tungsten-iron shotshells.

them, so the faster the shot travels to the target, the fewer times you will shoot behind birds. Still, the selection of shot type boils down to how confident you are shooting a particular load, and that is determined by trial and error.

The downside to the use of steel alternative nontoxic shot is cost. These shells are sold in boxes of 10 instead of the standard 25, and the

Jeff Petersen, Old Harbor, Alaska
"Use Tungsten/Iron and Hevishot"

After years of experimentation, Jeff Petersen, who guides for sea ducks off the rugged coast of Kodiak Island, has come up with what he thinks are the best loads for hard-to-kill ducks like eiders and scoters. "If you shoot 3½-inch shells, bring No. 2 shot in tungsten/iron. If you shoot 3-inch shells, bring No. 4 tungsten/iron or Hevishot. And if you shoot 2¾-inch shells, shoot number No. 6 Hevishot. Of course this is dependent on the species you are targeting. If you're targeting eiders, use the 3-inch, No. 4 tungsten/iron, and for harlequins use 2¾-inch, No. 6 Hevishot. I was strictly a No. 2 and BB, 3½-inch shell shooter when one of my clients proved to me he could kill any of the birds we have here with 3-inch shells using No. 4 tungsten/iron."

price of 10 shells is about the same as a box of 25 premium steel shot shells. The price may go down as more manufacturers enter the market, but the price of the components, particularly the shot itself, will probably always keep the cost significantly higher than steel. You'll have to decide if the performance justifies the additional cost. If your pocketbook is a limiting factor, then magnum or premium steel shot shells made by the major manufacturers will do the

Another non-toxic shot alternative.

job fine. If price is less important, go with the alternative to steel for top performance and knockdown power. If you use the alternatives, select shot sizes as if you were shooting lead—Nos. 4, 5, and 6 when shooting over decoys and Nos. 2 and 4 for long-distance shooting.

Shotgun chokes create as much debate as the best type of shot to use. The word choke refers to the constriction at the end of the shotgun barrel that determines the size of the shot pattern at a standard distance. Before the advent of steel shot, most waterfowl guns were choked full or modified. In the case of over-unders, the bottom barrel was modified and generally fired first, and the top barrel was full and fired second. Others preferred their doubles choked full and full. A full choke delivers a tighter pattern (smaller area of coverage) at 30 yards than a modified choke. The full choke was chosen for long shots when the pattern needs to stay tight for longer distances. The more open chokes, like improved-cylinder, deliver a wide pattern for close-in shooting but tend to scatter at longer distances and the pattern falls apart. Modified is the middle ground and performs well at closer distances and at moderate ranges. While this applies to lead and the steel alternatives, it does not apply to shooting steel shot shells.

Most steel shot manufacturers recommend using more open chokes for the best performance. The suggestion is based on field testing and patterning with factory guns and standard chokes. Generally, if you used a full choke with lead shot you should drop down to modified with steel shot, and if you primarily shot a gun choked modified, you would use improved-cylinder with steel. Because every gun, choke, shot size, and powder charge acts differently, however, the only way to know for sure is to pattern the shotgun and loads you normally use for duck hunting. When patterning, try several chokes and look for a uniform pattern at 30 yards. With the widespread use of screw-in chokes, it's easy to compare the performance of a standard load in the same gun with different chokes.

Screw-in chokes even allow changes in the field to match shooting conditions. I remember one cold December day in Maine, hunting eiders on a half-tide ledge in Penobscot Bay. I thought the birds would be swinging wide over the decoys, so I put a modified choke in my pump gun. I was surprised when the eiders came rocking in with feet down less than 20 yards out. After a couple of misses at close range, it was apparent my gun was over-choked for the situation at hand. I quickly changed the choke tube from modified to improved-cylinder. The results were dramatic. The eiders continued to decoy at close range, but now they were centered in the pattern and the number of clean kills increased.

Screw-in choke tubes.

Other Shotgun Features

When I bought my first shotgun in the 1960s, they came in one flavor of barrel and stock finish—high-gloss bluing and an oil-finished wood stock. Today the choices are far greater, with special-purpose models for waterfowling offering specialty finishes, synthetic stocks, and slings. Among the most popular innovations are the finishes that replaced the standard high-gloss bluing. Sure there are plenty of blued shotguns out there, but more and more duck hunters are buying guns with camouflage finishes. Turkey hunters were the first to cover their guns with camouflage tape or socks to mask high-gloss stocks and barrels. Waterfowl hunters soon discovered they could benefit from doing the same. It wasn't long before the major manufacturers developed camouflage finishes and offered them to the consumer. Your gunsmith or a manufacturer's custom shop may also be able to apply a camouflage finish to almost any shotgun. A camouflage finish might prevent only a few birds from flaring during a season, but on that day it could make the difference between success and failure.

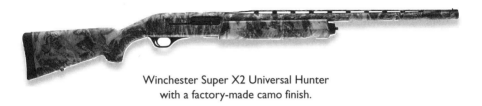

Winchester Super X2 Universal Hunter
with a factory-made camo finish.

In addition to camouflage finishes, some field-grade shotguns come with a matte finish that is essentially nonglare bluing. Teflon finishes are another alternative designed to repel water and prevent metal parts from rusting. Your gunsmith can apply them but the process is expensive.

Most shotguns still have wood stocks and forearms. In recent years, the use of synthetic or plastic stocks has increased. The stocks are weatherproof and won't crack, chip, or scratch. For some hunters, a plastic stock is not as pleasing to the eye as a natural wood stock. Some people also claim they don't feel the same as a wood stock when they are brought to the shoulder. I find them practical—but again the choice of stock material is a personal preference.

Most 12-gauge factory-made shotguns come with a recoil pad. Affixed to the butt of the stock, a recoil pad is designed to dampen the recoil generated by the shotgun blast. This is particularly important when using magnum waterfowl loads. If your shotgun does not have a recoil pad, I suggest you get one installed by a gunsmith. When you get measured for the pad, bring your duck-hunting coat so the gunsmith can calculate the proper length of the stock based on the clothes you wear in the field.

At one time, field-grade shotguns came with or without a ventilated rib. Today, very few, if any, factory shotguns are available without a rib. A ventilated rib is designed to provide the shooter with a sighting plane that extends from the receiver to the tip of the barrel. This sighting plane makes tracking a moving target easier and adds a pleasing look to the barrel.

Before the advent of interchangeable chokes, the 30-inch barrel was a favorite of many waterfowl hunters. The long barrel, generally choked full, provides a long sighting plane and the momentum for a smooth, sustained swing. Today, with screw-in chokes widely available in factory guns and many shooters going to faster-swinging shotguns, most waterfowl hunters buy shotguns with 28- or 26-inch barrels. The 28-inch is probably the best all-around choice for diving and sea duck hunters, who have a tendency to shoot in more open situations and at longer ranges than many puddle duck hunters.

The use of slings, long popular with rifle hunters, has become more widespread among waterfowl hunters. As with camouflage finishes, turkey hunters were the first to use slings to carry their shotguns to the hunting area. Likewise, waterfowl hunters often walk long distances and have found a sling makes the journey more comfortable and frees up your hands to carry shell bags, decoys, or a heavy strap of ducks. Many special-purpose shotguns come with a sling, but if your gun doesn't have one, you can install one yourself or have a gunsmith do it. I have found woven web slings more useful in the wet conditions encountered when waterfowl hunting than the more expensive leather slings.

Shotgun cleaning is likely one of the most important aspects of a day afield, yet it is one of the things that is put off the most. If you want your shotgun (particularly semi-autos) to stay in good working order and look halfway decent, it must be cleaned. After every outing, wipe down your shotgun with a rag to remove any moisture, mud, or foreign matter. Spray the meal parts with WD-40 or a similar product.

WD-40 is a penetrating liquid that displaces water. After the gun has been sprayed and wiped down, give it a once-over with an oily rag to coat the metal parts and prevent rusting. Part way through the season, or after particularly hard use where water and mud are involved, I take my shotgun apart and give it a thorough cleaning. This includes running a cleaning rod down the bore to remove powder residues, cleaning the trigger mechanism, removing and cleaning screw-in chokes. In autoloaders and pumps, I also clean the bolt and magazine tube. Wipe down the stock and oil the metal parts and you're ready to go.

A quality gun case is a must for transporting your shotgun to and from the field.

If you own a shotgun, you should own a gun case. If you don't, go out and buy one. When transporting a firearm, many states require that it not only be unloaded but also cased. A case also protects your shogun from scratches, dents, and general abuse during transport. Dozens of types and materials are used to make gun cases. I like Cordura nylon cases for their durability, and padded cases for the protection they afford. Gun socks are useful but do not give the degree of protection found in a gun case. If your case has been in the bottom of the boat getting wet, don't put your shotgun in it, zip it up, and leave it. In no time your gun will be covered with rust. And don't put a wet shotgun in a dry case. Before casing your shotgun, dry it off. Once you reach home, store your shotgun uncased.

Improving Your Shooting Skill

Shooting skill is a combination of natural ability and practice. The more opportunities a person has to fire a shotgun at game—paying attention to what works and what doesn't—the faster he or she will become a better shot. To increase the practice portion of shooting, many hunters spend time on the sporting clays course to sharpen their eye. Sporting clays simulates hunting situations more than skeet or trap. Have an experienced shooter stand behind you on the sporting clays range to help determine what you are doing right and what you are doing wrong. This will help accelerate the learning curve. You will achieve even more improvement by attending a certified shooting school like those offered by Orvis.

Becoming a good shot requires real in-the-field shooting experience—and plenty of off-the-field target practice.

Longer shots require a longer lead. Determining just how much might be better left to instinct than to analytical calculations.

The first step in becoming a good shot is to purchase a shotgun that "feels" good when you bring it to your shoulder and look down the sighting plane. Factory shotguns are made for the average shooter. Most factory guns work fine as long as you are close to that average, but if you have long or short arms, are tall or short, or have a slight or heavy-set build, the standard gun dimensions may not fit you, and your shooting will suffer. The way to overcome this is to have your shotgun custom fitted. The fine custom doubles all come with a fitting where a gunsmith takes measurements and fashions a stock that is tailor-made for you. A gunsmith can take a factory gun, do the measurements, and fit the shotgun to you. It's not a custom-made stock, but it will fit you far better than an out-of-the-box factory gun. The cost is relatively small and most gunsmiths perform the task.

Be patient and let the ducks work within effective shooting range before you fire your shotgun.

Once you have purchased a shotgun that feels comfortable and fits and you have spent a few days on the sporting clay course, it's time to hit the marshes. When hunting ducks it's important to let the birds get in close before firing. One of the most frustrating things for new and seasoned shooters alike is hunting with someone who invariably shoots at the edge of the effective range. Let the birds work! If most of your shots are inside 35 yards, the number of birds you bag per shells fired will go up significantly compared to the ratio at shots greater than 40 yards. And for new shooters, in particular, success is what keeps them coming back.

Every bird you shoot requires a different lead based on speed, angle of approach, and how close the bird is to you. A bird that passes directly overhead may require a fast swing, but at the point it passes directly overhead, it may require very little lead. The same is true for a bird that is backpedaling with wings cupped and feet down ready to land in the decoys. This bird need only be blocked out with your gun barrel—very little lead is required. In contrast, a duck 40 yards out and passing left to right at full speed may require several feet of lead.

So how do you determine how much to lead a bird? Very few birds are missed because the shot pattern is in front of the target. Most birds are missed because the shot is behind them. A common example that any diver or sea duck hunter can give you is shooting a bird coming in low over the water and leading the bird with the intent of hitting the bird dead center. But when you pull the trigger, your shot string hits the water two feet behind the bird and you may even drop the next bird in line.

Determining lead comes from an internal computer that, as you shoulder your shotgun, takes into account speed and distance to the target, angle of approach, wind speed, and direction. Collectively, this automatic analysis of the shooting situation is called instinct. If I don't shoulder my shotgun until a split second before I shoot, I'm able to find the target, attain the proper lead, and shoot from instinct. The result is that I drop more ducks than if I think about the shot too much. If I shoulder the shotgun and track the bird coming in, I have more of a tendency to overanalyze the lead and miss.

Another shooting method is generally called sustained lead. This style of shooting requires a lead that begins ahead of the bird and is sustained by the proper barrel swing until the shot is fired. Finally, the swing-through method requires the shooter to swing the barrel from behind the bird, catch up with the target, and swing past it. As the muzzle passes the bird, the trigger is pulled. All three methods are effective, and with practice you will determine which one is best for you. Remember, also, to pick a single target when a group of ducks comes into range. Flock shooting is a common mistake, but a good shot will pick a single bird, shoulder, swing, and fire.

Confidence is as important as anything and can only be gained by doing a task over and over again. Everybody has his or her own skill level when it comes to any endeavor, and shooting is no different. The goal is to reach your full potential, and while you'll never drop every duck that presents itself, you'll start to bag enough birds to gain the personal satisfaction that is right for you.

PLANNING A
DUCK HUNTING TRIP

Psychologists have discovered that each personal experience can be divided into three parts. The same paradigm applies well to duck hunting. One-third of the experience is the value of anticipation—looking forward to the hunt, planning, getting your gear ready, buying new equipment, and traveling to the area. Another one-third is the participation value—the hunt itself, the thrill of the chase, seeing a flock of canvasbacks power into the decoys, and the shot that anchors a handsome drake. The final one-third is the value of reflection on the experience and what happened after the hunt—telling your buddies back at work about

At least a third of the enjoyment is in the anticipation and build-up before the shooting even starts.

the hunt, looking at photos, and savoring grilled duck hot off the barbecue. It takes all three parts to make a complete experience. This chapter deals primarily with the anticipation portion of the experience but touches on the other aspects, as well.

One of my most memorable duck hunts took more planning than most. It was a waterfowl hunt south of the border, down Mexico way, that two buddies and I put together right after I got out of the navy in 1970. I had earlier read a magazine article or two (which I dutifully saved) about the great hunting Mexico had to offer. We were an adventurous lot and, while I spoke only limited Spanish at the time, it seemed like the ultimate duck hunting adventure. We lived near Los Angeles, and while the west coast of Mexico was far, it was reachable. One of the magazine articles had indicated that I'd need a Mexican hunting license and gun permits. The article gave the name of an individual at a sporting goods store who could obtain the necessary papers. A short drive and an hour of conversation later, I had the paperwork for a Mexican hunting license in hand. We also narrowed down the region we wanted to hunt to an area near Los Mochis in the state of Sinaloa. I researched the area the best I could, contacting the Mexican Tourism Department, talking to veterans of Mexican hunting trips, and obtaining maps.

Our licenses and gun permits arrived a month later, and during our Christmas break from college we hit the road in my pickup, with a boat on top of the camper, shells, shotguns, decoys, and a sense of adventure. The 1,000-mile journey took a couple of days, but we finally arrived in Los Mochis, found a reasonably priced motel, and inquired at the front desk if anyone knew about duck hunting. To our surprise the answer was yes. The desk attendant made a telephone call, and thirty minutes later a round-faced guy in his forties showed up at our motel room. He introduced himself in English as Joe. We agreed on a hunt the next day for redheads and bluebills at a saltwater estuary south of town. To make a long story short, the weeklong trip was an unqualified success and the shooting for both divers and puddle ducks was outstanding. We saw no other hunters during the week, could shoot wherever we wanted, were greeted with open arms by the people,

---

John Reid, Detroit, Michigan
"Watch the Weather"

"**I**'ve found that some of my best shooting occurs just before a front moves through," advises John Reid, who hunts divers on Lake St. Clair at least thirty days during the season. "New birds arrive the day before and the day the front reaches us. Ducks traveling ahead of the front are tired and hungry and are, therefore, much easier to decoy than birds that have been around for several weeks. I watch the local weather with great interest, and when a front is on the way, I take a day off work and hunt ducks."

---

and enjoyed some of best duck hunting I've ever experienced. For the next fifteen years, two buddies and I made the annual pilgrimage to Los Mochis to hunt with Joe.

The moral of the story is: If your planning includes good research and you have a sense of adventure, there are many excellent locations that even today offer quality hunting. Many can be planned on your own, and with the advent of the Internet, faxes, and cell phones, setting up a hunting trip has become even easier.

It's worth noting just how valuable a tool the Internet is in planning a trip. One of the first things a hunter new to an area should do is contact the Web site of the wildlife department or DNR in the state or Canadian province he will be visiting. While the sites vary in the amount of information presented, they all provide information on seasons, bag limits, and the cost of licenses and stamps. Some provide information on their state-operated hunting areas, as well as harvest information. A few even provide the e-mail addresses of biologists and waterfowl researchers. These people can be contacted, and if you don't

For waterfowlers who want to get the most out of a hunt, especially in unfamiliar territory, a good guide service can be well worth the extra cost.

take up too much of their time, they will often answer questions regarding species available, timing of migrations, and other key bits of information. You will find links to all fifty states and the Canadian provinces at www.fishandwildlife.org.

Another important contact is the U.S. Fish and Wildlife Service (202-208-4131; www.fws.gov). They are responsible for the management of migratory birds in the United States and operate 540 national wildlife refuges in all fifty states. More than 311 of these refuges allow hunting and currently about 235 allow waterfowl hunting. The refuges have biologists who will often answer questions and many national wildlife refuges maintain their own Web sites.

Other federal public agencies also have public lands open to hunting, including the U.S. Forest Service (www.fs.fed.us), Bureau of Land Management (www.blm.gov), Bureau of Reclamation (www.usbr.gov), U.S. Army Corps of Engineers (www.usace.army.mil), and Tennessee Valley Authority (www.tva.gov). There also is a Web site (www.recreation.gov) that provides information on recreation (including hunting) on all public lands in the United States. The site is useful and offers a wealth of information, including directions and phone numbers.

The counterpart to the U.S. Fish and Wildlife Service in Canada is the Canadian Wildlife Service. They can provide information on

Capt. Jeff Coats, Bel Air, Maryland
"Preparing Scoters"

Capt. Jeff Coats specializes in early season sea duck hunting on Chesapeake Bay. "One of the most frequent questions I get from my hunters is—'After we shoot 'em, what do we do with them?' First, I breast the scoters as soon as possible after they are shot, and then—this is the important part—I remove EVERY bit of fat. Once the fat is removed, I wash the breasts thoroughly and soak them in salt water overnight. The next day I prepare them fresh like I would any other duck that has been breasted. The unpleasant taste often found in sea ducks is in the fat."

waterfowl throughout Canada. Contact the Canadian Wildlife Service at 800-668-6767 or 819-997-2800; www.cws.ca. Also be aware that a temporary import permit is required to bring firearms into Canada, and handguns are prohibited. Nonresidents traveling to Canada with firearms are required to present a Firearms Declaration Form (JUS 909 EF) at customs. The document is available by calling 800-731-4000 or by downloading a copy from the Canadian Firearms Centre Web site (www.cfc.gc.ca). The document is also available from Canadian Customs upon entering the country, but you will save time if you already have the form filled out. The customs officer will verify the firearms listed and witness your signature before issuing a declaration. Currently, there is a $50 Canadian fee. The declaration acts as a temporary license and is valid for sixty days. To buy ammunition in Canada, you must have a confirmed declaration.

In addition to public agency Web sites, there are dozens of private sites maintained for hunters. Many of them offer products for sale, while others have chat rooms, track migrations, and offer online waterfowl hunting articles and technical tips. To locate these, go to a search engine like Google (www.google.com) or Yahoo (www.yahoo.com) and type in "waterfowl hunting." You'll get plenty of sites to visit. The Internet is also valuable in checking weather conditions—both current and seven- or ten-day forecasts. Among the most popular sites are The Weather Channel (www.weather.com) and AccuWeather (www.accuweather.com).

In the past thirty years there has been a proliferation of professional hunting guides in virtually every area where waterfowl are found. Today much of the planning can be left to your guide or outfitter. Some guided trips are expensive and include airfare, food, lodging, and guide service. Others are reasonably priced and may include guide service only. For hunters who have precious little spare time and want to get the most out of a hunt, particularly in an unfamiliar area, hiring

Brenda Haley, Waldo, Maine
"Eider Cuisine"

"**M**any of our waterfowl hunters ask if eiders are fit to eat," says Brenda Haley of Coastal Maine Outfitters. "My answer is yes! Here's how to do it. Breast the birds and soak them overnight in a strong baking soda–water solution. Then cut the breast meat into 1-inch cubes, place in a skillet, and blanch in milk for three or four minutes. Drain off the milk, which in the blanching process removes much of the 'gamey' taste. Rinse, and then sauté the meat along with chopped onions, butter, a cup of red wine, and a dash of rosemary and tarragon. Simmer for five to seven minutes. Serve with a sweet-and-sour sauce. The result is amazing!"

a guide is a solid investment. Many guides and outfitters have Web sites that provide a full description, including prices for their hunts. Still it's important to realize that not every guided hunt is successful, but the probability for a reasonably good hunt increases substantially. But even on a guided hunt, bluebird days, missed migrations, and access problems can make a hunt difficult.

I have been fortunate to hunt waterfowl in a dozen foreign countries, including numerous trips to Mexico and Canada and at least twenty of the forty-nine states that allow waterfowl hunting (Hawaii is the exception). Still, I continue to look for new and interesting locations and return to time-tested areas. If a hunter is so inclined, he can hunt waterfowl virtually year-round. You can start the year during early September in Canada or Alaska, then follow-up with a season that opens in early October in the upper Midwest. Once your area has frozen-up and the birds move south, you can do the same and hunt in the southern portion of the United States. Here, the shooting is good until the season closes in late January. Then if you book a trip to Mexico, you can hunt ducks until the season closes in early March. If you still haven't had enough, the duck season in South America (Argentina and Uruguay have the best duck hunting) opens in May and runs until August. Before you know it, September is here again and waterfowl hunting in Canada and Alaska is back on tap.

For winter diver hunting, head to Louisiana or other parts of the Deep South.